BETTINA DEDA

Downsize with Style

A 5-Step Process to Create a
Happy Home and Refine Your New Lifestyle

A CIP catalogue of this book is available from the National Library of Australia.

Deda, Bettina

First Printing, 2014
Downsize with Style
ISBN 978-0-9924013-0-6

Printed in Australia

Designer: Sanela Hromadzic
Illustrator: Joaquín Gonzalez Dorao

Contents

Foreword   5

Author's Note   8

What do I have?   19
INVENTORY, PRIORITISING, SAYING GOODBYE

Step 1: De-clutter and Tidy Up   20

What do I need?   39
DECORATING ESSENTIALS AND WISH LIST

Step 2: Find Your Personal Decorating Style   54

What do I want?   69
DREAM BIG, BE CREATIVE, MIX & MATCH

Step 3: Visualise Your Ideas   70

Step 4: Layout Your Space   78

Step 5: Start Decorating   122

Tips & tricks   149
TO MAKE DOWNSIZING EASIER AND MORE FUN

A final word: 176
BE TRUE TO YOUR DECORATING STYLE

Foreword

My name is Lorraine Cox and I feel very honoured to be asked to write the foreword to this exciting and insightful book *Downsize with Style*.

I am a downsizing and removal consultant, specialising in helping people when they are moving from the family home into beautiful retirement and lifestyle resorts.

Having owned and run a successful downsizing business for over ten years, and before that run a removal company for ten years, I have seen hundreds of people downsize from the family home. Those two businesses now work hand in hand helping people to downsize and move with as minimal an amount of stress as possible.

I met Bettina through a women's business group we were both involved in, and we found we had much in common, particularly in wanting to help people when they had decided to downsize to smaller homes. Like many people (especially women!), who are passionate about what they do, there is always much to talk about and not a lot a room to stop for a breath.

One of the times we met to discuss this book Bettina had her young son with her. I had sponsored Max a few weeks before in a fundraising event, A Week Without Words. He and his friends were raising money to help a local school that assists children with additional needs, and their quest was to stay silent for eight hours, which was an amazing feat. I was happy to sponsor this thoughtful young man.

After I left our meeting that day, I had to laugh, as I thought, this poor child was totally silent during our entire meeting as he could not get a word in edgeways between these two passionate women and their talk of downsizing. It would have been an easy way for him to make a few more dollars for his charity, without even trying!

Even though we could be seen as competitors in the field of downsizing – myself from the area of assisting with the moving process, and making the move as stress-free as possible, and Bettina from the area of helping her clients enjoy the process of downsizing and making their new home, although smaller, stylish and beautiful to move in to – I think we complement each other perfectly.

Bettina's philosophy of life is one of gratitude, which sits very comfortably with my values and how I try to live my own life. I loved reading about how she came to those beliefs.

When her clients decide to downsize, she works with them to make this transition the joyful and happy experience it should be.

Bettina's book has hit the nail on the (decorating) head, so to speak. Downsizing to an apartment does not mean downsizing on style, and her knowledge of colour and making small spaces work is exciting.

We see many people downsize when sometimes their heart is really not in it, but with the practical and emotional help that Bettina offers, this transition can be made so much easier.

On the other hand, there are the people who are so excited at the thought of getting rid of their large home and having a small home to maintain that will fit in with their busy lifestyles. They may not have the attachment to their goods, like some people, but they still want to have a stylish and practical smaller home to live in. Bettina's book, and help, can only add to that excitement.

The detail she goes into with her ideas of starting to de-clutter makes me want to run and look through my cupboards and start doing some de-cluttering of my own. I can picture it as I read her steps to take, and she makes it seem easy, even fun!

While giving practical advice, Bettina also captures the emotion that goes with 'getting rid' off much loved items. She tackles that emotional side with grace and style, very much like herself.

I may have been helping people move for almost 20 years, and I thought I had a lot of the answers to help my clients trying to downsize, but I think I had only just touched the tip of the iceberg with many of my ideas.

Downsize with Style has opened my eyes to many other solutions that will enable me to help my clients, and I think this book will become my second bible when helping them through the process of making that move into a retirement and lifestyle village.

I wish Bettina every success with her book *Downsize with Style* because it is clear that it is written with a lot of love and passion, which comes from her very grateful heart.

Lorraine Cox

Author's Note

Beauty and Gratitude

I would like to start this book with two things that are very important to me: beauty and gratitude. Ever since I was a child I loved to surround myself with beautiful things. I remember collecting beautiful shells and stones while on holidays with my parents. In my teens I loved beautiful vibrant colours, handbags and shoes (of course!). When I moved into my first tiny apartment I started buying beautiful homewares to decorate my place. I always was drawn to beautiful art, and started painting in 2005. I need beauty around me on a daily basis. I need it to work, to be creative and to feel good. It makes me happy when I come in my bathroom in the morning and see a beautiful flower standing on my windowsill. I love my beautiful feather collection, my artworks and inspirational pictures on a mood board in my office, or the breathtaking nature on Sydney's Northern Beaches.

Only in 2012, after reading the book *Inspiring Courageous Leaders* by Mandy Holloway, did I find out that beauty is one of my top three values. This gave me clarity as to why beauty has always been, and is still, so important for me. And it is not only important on a personal level: it drives my business every day.

The other important thing I would like to share with you, is gratitude. Gratitude is the second of my top values. I believe gratitude is one of the most important pillars of joy (by the way, *The Gospel of Joy* is a great book by Amanda Gore). I was taught to say thank you and being grateful by my parents and grandmother. I remember my grandmother talking about how she survived two World Wars in Germany, the second with five little children to

feed – when there was no food available. She once said to me that she hopes that I never have to go through this experience, and that I should be very grateful to live in a part of the world where people don't have to suffer from a war being waged in their own country. This is something I will never forget.

I practise gratitude every day. A good way to do it, is a gratitude journal. Write down every night what you have been grateful for on that day. This is a great way to reflect on your day. I also teach my boys to be grateful for what they have experienced during their day, even if negative things happened to them. I believe that you should be grateful for anything that happens to you, as nothing happens without a reason.

'Gratitude is not only the greatest of virtues, but the parent of all the others.'

– Cicero

I am very grateful for how my life changed after our family moved from Germany to Australia in 2008. It was a big step for me as I left everything behind: my parents, my friends, our house (which we had only renovated a few years before), and my career in public relations. But without having stepped out of my comfort zone, I would have never found my true passion in life: interior styling.

I am an interior stylist, designer, artist, colour lover and born organiser. I love to help homeowners create a happy home and lifestyle through beautiful and inspiring interiors. I believe that only in a home with heart and personality, a home that reflects your personal decorating style, can you truly relax and reinvigorate your (apartment) lifestyle. Your home should be a space that you love to come home to every day.

Embrace the Change

Downsizing is often associated with negative feelings and emotions. I would like to encourage you to see it differently. Live with an attitude of gratitude, gratitude for the life you have lived, and the time you spent with your family and friends in your family home. To start a new chapter of your life, you need to step out of your comfort zone and be ready to experience new and exciting things.

The idea for this book was born when I read about the major physical changes Australian cities are going through. More and more people prefer an urban lifestyle close to amenities. They choose to live in low maintenance apartments rather than big houses for various reasons: simplifying their lifestyle, saving money on furnishings, appliances and energy, gaining more time for travelling and hobbies, or downsizing to start a new chapter of their life.

Australia has currently six million people over 55 and by the end of the century this number will have risen to 16 million. With advanced health care services, the retiring generations of today, and the future, are more active and fit, and do not think about retirement villages in the traditional sense. At this stage of their lives they often want to start a new chapter and to be close to the city's buzz, meet friends in coffee shops, and be part of their community. Chris Johnson AM, Chief Executive Officer of Urban Task Force Australia, emphasizes that a new market of older people, downsizing from houses to apartments, often in the same suburb, is emerging.

The baby boomers – those born between 1945 and 1965 – are currently the largest age group. As they grow older they will change the normal age distribution in Australia's major cities. These baby boomers will downsize, preferably close to where they currently live, states the City Futures research group from the University of NSW. And they want great places to live that happen to suit their age requirements. If you are a baby boomer, it is likely you will want to downsize in the same area you currently live in.

The City Futures report notes that many boomer homeowners are sitting on valuable assets. They are approaching retirement with a financial position inextricably tied to their home and the asset it represents. As a result of this financial security they are more likely to have substantive aspirations for their post-retirement years. This period, termed the Third Age, lasts until a more frail old age is reached. The report further explains that, because this period of lifestyle and identity reinvention has not been experienced before, it is a very significant factor. Baby boomers could spend up to one third of their life in the Third Age. The spending and lifestyle patterns of this life stage are largely unknown, as are the demands on infrastructure and services (*Urban Ideas Magazine*, May 2013).

5 Steps to *Downsize with Style*

Talking to clients and prospects about the biggest challenges when downsizing, three major topics emerged:

* Defining your new lifestyle

* De-cluttering and prioritising what to keep

* Storage optimisation in a smaller space.

Can you relate to these challenges? Are you procrastinating your downsizing project because you are overwhelmed and don't know where to start? Are you waking up in the middle of night because you are not sure what furniture to keep and what to do with all the other things you can't take with you? Are you overwhelmed by the idea of starting again from scratch to create an inspiring and cosy home in a smaller space?

Don't worry you are not alone! If you keep reading this book, I will guide you through my easy-to-follow 5-step process *Downsize with Style*.

The five steps include

1. De-clutter and tidy up
2. Find your personal style
3. Visualise your ideas
4. Layout your space
5. Start decorating

You will learn how to overcome procrastination by working with a plan, checklists, and practical tips along the way. You will discover creative ways of recycling and free cycling (passing on beloved things to people who really appreciate them), how to identify your decorating essentials, how to enhance your personal style and how to awaken your creativity to achieve a stylish home without breaking the bank. You will have less stress while downsizing and be able to eventually refine your apartment lifestyle.

'Man cannot discover new oceans unless he has the courage to lose sight of the shore.'

– Andre Gide

Back in 1993 in Germany, when I worked in my first job in an editorial office, I got a crash course in downsizing and storage optimisation. My partner decided to separate from me (after we had moved in together) and I was forced to move out of our split-level open-plan 140 sqm luxury apartment to a tiny one-room place. It did not even have a separate bedroom! I remember sitting in this new apartment, in between my boxes piled up high under the ceiling, sobbing and wondering how on earth I would get all my stuff into this miniscule space. Well, I managed to do it by getting rid of things I no longer needed in the smaller space, and by choosing to keep a couple of inherited antique pieces and then transforming them into storage units for clothing and accessories. I used a shelving unit as a room divider between my tiny kitchen and sitting area. I furnished and decorated my place intuitively –

without any background in interior design, and long before I even thought of working in the industry. I fell back on my innate love of decorating and creating interesting vignettes.

Only when taking the big step of moving to Australia in 2008 did I discover my passion for colour and interiors. I started studying at a design school and finally found what I was really passionate about: helping homeowners to create beautiful and inspiring interiors with heart and personality. Spaces where they can truly relax and re-energise!

How to Get Started

As a born organiser I love lists and plans, and could not juggle my daily life without them. So, if you are about to downsize to a smaller space, sit down and make a plan. Ask yourself three questions:

* What do I have?
* What do I need?
* What do I want?

With this in mind start working on your downsizing strategy – step by step. Breathe deeply and relax. Follow my 5-step process to overcome procrastination and do one thing at a time.

You will discover how to:

* Simplify your life
* Stay organised
* Achieve a stylish interior in your home.

See downsizing as a step towards a new chapter of your life. In the following pages you will learn how to enhance your personal decorating style and save your wallet along the way. You don't have to spend a fortune to create a cosy home or sacrifice interior style when you are on a budget.

Embrace the future and the positive side of your new apartment lifestyle! Be grateful for your past experiences and the opportunities that lie ahead. Detach from negative emotions. Focus on gratitude and cheerful enthusiasm about your future in your new home.

This book will show you how to downsize with style, create a happy home and reinvigorate your apartment lifestyle.

Bettina

'I am going to make
everything around me beautiful –
that will be my life.'

– Elsie de Wolfe

What do i have?

INVENTORY, PRIORITISING, SAYING GOODBYE

Step 1: De-clutter and Tidy Up

You are planning to move to a smaller home or are in the process of downsizing already. Even if you are super-tidy and organised, you may face some de-cluttering challenges. For most of us, de-cluttering is not a favourite task and therefore frequently postponed. Do you wake up in the middle of the night, wondering how you can possibly manage to tidy up all your storage areas with everything else you are currently juggling? And do you always find a reason why today or this week is not the time to do it? Sound familiar? Well, relax and breathe deeply. Clutter builds up due to unresolved issues and unmade decisions. You are not alone, and your procrastination can be overcome by working with a plan and a strategy. You have already taken the first step by reading this book. If you follow my advice, you will learn an easy 3-step process to get over your procrastination and get your unpleasant jobs done – actually get anything done!

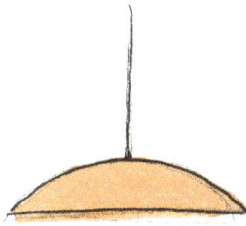

I learned this from a business coach who runs a very successful online business and provides tools to help you focus on the crucial things to move forward. This process can be applied to any project or task. I tried it and it works well for me. If you stick to it you will overcome procrastination, and show up and do what you have to do!

Three Proven Steps to Get Anything Done

1. Make it a priority!

On a scale from 1 to 10: how committed are you to your downsizing project? Think about this for a few minutes and write your answer on a piece of paper. Be honest with yourself. If you are not 100 percent committed to realising your project you won't get there! If you are truly committed to simplifying your life and downsizing to a smaller space you will achieve the results you want. And to achieve your desired outcome you need to start de-cluttering your family home! Clutter is a series of unmade (decorating) decisions. Start making decisions and you will reduce your clutter with ease.

As I said, this 3-step process works in all areas of your life. I offered my help for the set design of my son's class play. My job was to create a step for the stage, resembling a Greek column, for the children to stand on. After a brainstorming session with the teacher we decided that a piece of a tree trunk would be the perfect prop for the set. I left the school that day determined to find a tree trunk, and started some research. I contacted a nursery, and also asked a teacher from a preschool that had logs in their outdoor area. From this teacher I heard that she had found their logs by coincidence on a street in her suburb. The next morning when I drove my kids to the bus stop a whole pile of cut tree trunks was lying in one of the streets in our neighbourhood. I couldn't believe my eyes! What a great find! And it proved again that, if you are determined and committed, things fall in place.

2. Schedule it!

Once you are sure about your level of commitment, you need to allocate time to get it done. Schedule it in your calendar. Start with one room. Do it strategically and work through each room, one after the other.

Allocating time does not mean you have to do everything yourself. If you are too overwhelmed, hire a de-cluttering business to get the ball rolling.

3. Show up and do it!

How you do anything, is how you do everything! Now that you have made your downsizing project a priority and scheduled time to move forward, the most important step is to take action and do it. Show your 100 percent commitment whatever you do. Don't let yourself get distracted by other things. If you have planned to start de-cluttering, take a few hours or a day, and do it. You will be amazed what you discover when you do things you have never done before. Set yourself boundaries and, again, don't get distracted. Focus on what you want to do in your set time frame. I can guarantee that you will progress with your project every day.

Scenario

Barbara (60) and Brian (62) are finally getting closer to making the move from their family home to a smaller apartment. They are only moving a few kilometres away in the same area, but their family home is full of things accumulated over the past 30 years. They have not been able to downsize on their own even though they have been talking about it for years. There is still no definite moving date. They are both emotionally attached to most of their items. They have lots of boxes with papers from prior jobs and hobbies. They would prefer that their children take most of their things, so they said they could 'take what they want'. They are not very keen on going systematically through their rooms to de-clutter. Their children are willing to help, but do not want to take the majority of their parent's belongings.

The first step to successfully downsize is a 100 percent commitment to getting it done. Make a decision to make it a priority. See it as a chance to start a new chapter of your life. De-cluttering and sorting out your things is the first step of this journey. I recommend doing this step-by-step and room-by-room. Tackle one room at a time and follow my de-cluttering strategy. Do it together with your children, if they are offering their help. And accept that they most probably don't want to take away all your unwanted items.

To help you make decisions, think about what you would take if you could only take one thing from each box or drawer you are going through.

If you haven't used an item in the past year, chances are you don't really need it. Save a few of the things you are emotionally attached to and that really mean something to you, but bite the bullet and sell or donate the rest. The following pages provide a range of sources to pass on things to people who will appreciate them.

'Put your heart, mind and soul
into even your smallest acts.
This is the secret of success.'

- Swami Sivananda

If you are not able or willing to sort out each room systematically because it is too overwhelming, and you don't know where to start, I recommend seeking help from a professional de-cluttering business. Get three quotes and make a decision to invest in this service – it is probably much more costly to pack and move everything, and to have to pay for external storage when you can't fit all your belongings in your new space.

Acknowledge the fact that you can make the decision to downsize at this stage in your lives, and on your own terms, even if it is a daunting and difficult task. It will most probably be even more daunting in ten years time.

De-cluttering Strategy

Starting to de-clutter is the hardest part of your journey. There will always be stuff you can't throw out, even if you haven't touched it for years. Therefore, it is really helpful to look at this job as taking inventory and rethinking what to do with each item. Once you have committed to do your de-cluttering homework, do it strategically, work through it step by step and tackle one room at a time. Find creative ways of passing on things that won't fit in your new home.

Think of four piles and allocate each item to one of them:

1. Things that go straight in the bin

2. Items you can sell

3. Donations to charities, schools, community centres

4. Beloved treasures you want to keep.

Now, the important thing is to follow-up your de-cluttering sessions with actions. Once you have built your piles and finished with one room, take the rubbish to the waste management centre or organise a pick-up. Sell your 'for sale' items online (e.g. on eBay) or at a physical market. Research on your local council's website when markets are on. This, of course, requires time and effort, but if you are clever, you can earn money from your de-cluttering job!

I went with my son to a local kids' market, and together we made more than $400 selling my son's toys, board games and clothes. He was so enthusiastic about it that buyers kept commenting on his sales skills. We had a great day together, made some money from stuff he did not play with any longer and got a reward for the time and effort we allocated to de-clutter and tidy up his room. By the way, this is a fantastic way to teach your (grand) children, that money needs to be earned and does not come out of ATMs.

Take the 'donation' pile to a local charity shop. Or research local book fairs where you can donate your books. Call charity organisations for a pick up of larger items (the furniture must be in good condition). They are always grateful for donations, and the money goes to a good cause. If you deliver your donations to a shop, take the time to browse their store and be inspired! I can tell you from my own experience, that you can make fabulous finds there.

Another creative way to let go of things you can't throw out, is to put them in an 'outbox'. This can be a physical box or, for larger items, an area in your house, where you put all the things

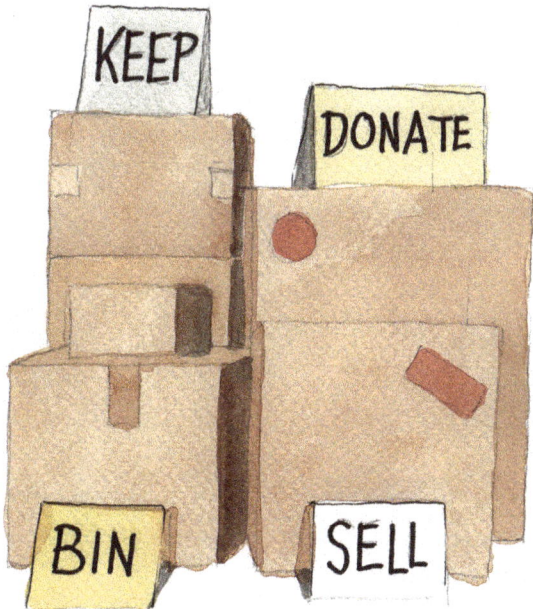

you want to get rid of. Leave them there for a week and see how you feel about them. If, after a week, you still think you want to keep the item put it on your pile to keep. For everything else, you have realised that you do not need it any longer, so give it away or trash it.

I love the term free cycling: passing things on to family, friends or other people to start a new life (check out www.freecycle.org). A creative way of free cycling is to create a donation tray or box in your entrance area, where you leave smaller items you would like to give away. Put larger items, that are in a good condition, at the curbside over the weekend with a sign 'For FREE' and offer them to all passers-by. You will be surprised how quickly your items will find new homes. Ask your visitors, neighbours, friends or your kids' friends to take something they like. Always remember: your trash could be someone else's treasure!

Another creative way to pass on beloved items is swap parties. If you have nice furniture or gorgeous homeware items you can't fit into your new (smaller) space, why not swap it for furniture or items you could use? What is very popular in the fashion industry, can also work for furniture and décor items. Invite some friends and ask them to bring photographs of furniture and homeware items they would like to swap. Make it as formal or casual you like, and keep it simple.

Offer your magazine collections to preschools or kindergartens for craft sessions, to a design school as a source for collage work (students need to cut out lots of images for their assignments), or to your doctor or hairdresser for their waiting areas.

You will feel better when you've completed this job. It frees up your mind and lets you focus on the exciting part of your creative journey: planning and decorating your new home.

To Do List

1. Make de-cluttering a priority!
2. Take inventory and start with one room
3. Create four piles
4. Follow-up with actions

Tips to De-clutter

I am not a professional organiser or de-cluttering specialist, but being a quite organised person with excellent time management skills, I recommend the following tips that work pretty well for me and keep my home tidy. And as I mentioned earlier, the most important thing to get anything done, is the 3-step process: Commit to it, schedule it, show up and do it! And don't forget, you don't have to do everything yourself! Outsourcing is always an option and sometimes the better choice.

Your paperwork

* Sort out mail before you even bring it in the house and throw all unwanted papers straight into your paper bin.

* Work with three trays on your desk: in-tray, bills to pay, filing, and instantly allocate each letter to one of the trays.

* Create a pin board in your kitchen (think of chalkboard paint) or use your fridge to remind you of important things you have to action in the next days.

* Batch activities around your paperwork: e.g. paying bills, filing papers, making phone calls, answering emails.

* Empty your email inbox once a week. Do it religiously and continuously. Create email folders where you archive your emails for easy retrieval.

Your kitchen cupboards and pantry

* Schedule times (twice a year) where you go through your cupboards, drawers and pantry. Empty and clean them.

* Organise under-sink cupboards with little baskets for

dishwashing liquid, cloths, brushes, rubber gloves etc.

* Divide your drawers with compartments for easy storage and sorting cutlery, kitchen accessories and other stuff you store in your kitchen.

* Go through your pantry on a regular basis. If you refill your pantry, check the expiry date of products that have been sitting there several months and dispose of them immediately, if they are expired.

* Group similar products, e.g. baking ingredients, pasta, rice and sauces, muesli and breakfast cereals, biscuits and crackers, and use small storage baskets for smaller items.

Your linen cupboard

* Empty your linen cupboard completely and take inventory.

* Allocate each piece to one of the four de-cluttering piles.

* Think about how many sets of bed linen you really need, and what is nice to have.

* Have dedicated shelves for your bed linen, towels, throws etc. to make sure everything goes back to the same place after washing. Label your shelves if that helps you to stay organised more easily.

* Learn how to fold a fitted sheet properly in order to maximise storage space. I never really got it right, until my mother-in-law showed me a few years ago.

* Organise your fitted sheets with the matching bed linen and flat sheet together in one pile. This looks great and gives you an instant overview of your colours and patterns when opening your cupboard.

* Buy gorgeous storage boxes (see Kikki-K, IKEA or Howard's

Storage World for fabulous finds) and store smaller items in labelled boxes.

Your wardrobe and accessories

* Use the same structure as above: schedule time to go through your wardrobe twice a year, for example spring and autumn.
* Empty your wardrobe and take inventory.
* Put each piece in one of the four de-cluttering piles.
* Once finished with this task, take action with each pile.
* Sort your clothes by pants (long and short), jackets, shirts, dresses, skirts etc. and find a dedicated space for them in your wardrobe. Group long- and short-sleeve T-shirts, jumpers, skirts, dresses.
* You can additionally sort your wardrobe by colours. This not only looks great, but also gives you an instant overview of the colours you have.
* For smaller items, use wardrobe organisation systems.
* Label your storage boxes or shelves and keep your items in the same place.
* Display your favourite jewellery on hooks or pin boards and make them a feature in your bedroom.
* Make a list of items you need to restock for the new season.
* Turn your wardrobe makeover into a fun event by organising a swap party.

Your garage

* Depending how much stuff you have stored in your garage over the years, it might be a good idea to hire a professional

to de-clutter your garage. Usually, there is hard work and heavy pieces involved and you should compare the cost of outsourcing to the time and effort you would need to invest in getting this space sorted.

* A general tip is to review this space on a continuous basis and not let too much clutter build up over time.

* Otherwise, work with large shelving units and closed cupboards and use the same principle as with the linen cupboard: group items (e.g. car accessories and cleaning, bike stuff, outdoor toys, tools, paint pots, garden equipment), sort them in large storage boxes (labelled) and allocate them to dedicated spaces.

'Design is a constant challenge
to balance comfort with luxe,
the practical with the desirable.'

– Donna Karan

Where to donate

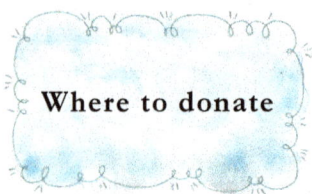

Lifeline: www.lifeline.org.au

The Salvation Army: www.salvationarmy.org.au/welcome/

St. Vincent de Paul Society: www.vinnies.org.au/home-act

Australian Red Cross: www.redcross.org.au

Local schools

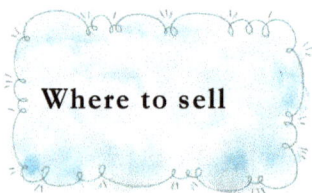

Where to sell

www.ebay.com.au

www.gumtree.com.au

www.tradingpost.com.au

www.simpletrade.com.au

www.locanto.com.au

www.melbourneexchange.com.au

www.cairnstrader.com

www.broometrader.com.au

Local antique and second hand shops (browse www.yellowpages.com.au)

Auction centres

Local markets

Where to swap

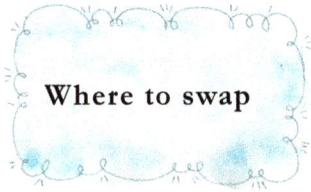

www.clothingexchange.com.au

www.recycleaustralia.swapace.com

www.u-exchange.com/barteraustralia

www.locanto.com.au

www.barter.freeadsaustralia.com

Where to recycle

www.ozrecycle.com

www.recyclingnearyou.com.au

www.mobilemuster.com.au

What do i need?

DECORATING ESSENTIALS AND WISH LIST

Keep the Essentials

Every home needs some basic pieces of furniture as a solid foundation to build on. As empty nesters you are going to start a new chapter of your life so you need to prioritise and decide which pieces are the most important to keep. And, what is missing. To know what you need to simplify your life and to create a happy home at the same time, you need to know what the basics are.

This is a list of essential pieces to start decorating, the foundation on which you add your personal touches to create a cosy and happy home.

These are your must-haves to get started in a smaller space:

Entrance/hall

* Chest of drawers for storage options
* Hallstand or wardrobe for jackets, bags, umbrellas, etc.
* Mirror
* Bench or seat

Living area

* 2–3 seater lounge
* 2 occasional chairs
* Coffee table (with storage option)
* Alternative: ottoman (with storage option)
* 2 small side tables
* Display cabinet for your treasured collections

* Bookshelf
* Standing light
* Entertainment unit

Dining area

* Dining table (4-seater)
* Dining chairs or benches
* Sideboard

Bedroom

* Bedside tables
* Reading lights
* Ottoman for seating and additional storage
* Wardrobe
* Washing basket

Bathroom

* Wall hung storage unit
* Stool

Study/guest bedroom

* Small desk with chair
* Sofa bed
* Open shelf
* Chest of drawers

Your Decorating Foundation

In this chapter we are focussing on the most important pieces of furniture to start a new chapter of your life in a smaller space. But don't worry, I encourage you to dream big and to add the icing on the cake later. We all have to work to a budget, and therefore it is vital to concentrate on the essentials first. You will find out that in order to create a home with heart and personality, you do not have to invest in designer pieces only. The trick is to be creative and courageous and to mix and match different price points, styles and textures, and, most importantly, to add your personality to your space.

You have most probably been to a friend's house and envied their interior. Everything seems to be perfect, a cosy and personal home, inviting and inspiring to others. And you wonder how someone can achieve such an outcome without hiring an interior designer. Well, I am pretty sure that this friend has the basics covered and understands how to layout a room, how to decorate with colour and texture and how to work with focal points. If you keep on reading this book, you will soon be starting to decorate and create an enviable and stylish outcome as well!

You have mastered the hardest part already: you have de-cluttered, donated and passed on items you can't take with you. You know what basic pieces you need to start decorating your new home. Now you are going to fill the gaps. You will create a solid foundation to start building a happy home and reinvigorate your apartment lifestyle.

Stay Organised in Style

Now it is time to get organised in style and start working with a project folder, a nice and stylish project folder that inspires you (check out Kikki-K for gorgeous organisers). This folder will carry all your lists, your papers and inspirations sorted by the different rooms: kitchen/dining, living room, master bedroom, bathroom etc. Collect all your notes, ideas, quotes, colour swatches and fabric samples in this folder. It will help you to stay organised and instantly find relevant material you need for your decorating project.

I am a very organised person and I love lists. They help me to stay focussed and prioritise. And it makes you feel good and in control of your project if you can tick off items from your list. I could not live without my lists with all the different things that go on in my daily life. We (especially the women in the house) are all required to be experts in multitasking and juggling household, family commitments, kids, schools, work … This is why I urge you to work with lists.

The first thing that goes into your folder is your written list of all the items that have survived your de-cluttering project. These are your starting points for your new home.

Additionally, you should compile a list of all the things you need to start decorating your new space. This is the list to fill any gaps you have in your essential decorating pieces, not a wish list of items you always wanted to buy. Carry your lists in a little notebook in your handbag, so that you can refer to them while shopping. Focus on what you need and keep in mind that you don't want to start cluttering your new space again with too many pieces you can't fit in a smaller space.

The third list is my favourite one: DREAM BIG and add all the pieces you would love to have. Brainstorm your DREAM HOME! What would you love to have, even if you can't afford it right now? I am talking about this absolutely stunning designer chair that you always wanted, but never bought, because of the kids, the pets and so on.

At this stage it can become quite frustrating when you compare your available space, and what you actually need to create a stylish home in a smaller space, with your wish list. Now it is time to prioritise! Think about what suits your lifestyle and where you need quality products that have a special functionality or feature.

And this is the reason why all these lists are so important. They will help you stay focussed on what you need and prevent you from buying the wrong pieces that won't fit in your new space. And you will know exactly what you are saving up for, if this stunning designer chair is becoming the focal point in your living area.

Invest in Classic Pieces and Quality

Spending on quality furniture for your home is a long-term investment. It is something that you buy for years, not just for one season. As you decided to start a new chapter of your life, why not go for some great designer pieces, recognising quality craftsmanship and materials, for your home? These feature pieces will stand the test of time, add a classic and sophisticated look to your home and show your sense of style. Then add your personal touch through décor and accessories, your treasured collections and books. This is what makes a house a home. *In Step 5 - Start Decorating* you will discover how to decorate a bookshelf and create eye-catching vignettes that become a conversation starter.

When considering your essential pieces, think of classic and quality in the first place. Then, be courageous and creative, and start mixing and matching what you love. Some people might find it popular to furnish and decorate their homes from top to bottom in designer furniture to achieve a look they have seen in a magazine. Others know all too well that a cleverly mixed interior is much more personal and inspiring – for themselves and others. It is comparable to the woman who dresses herself with a clever mix of classic designer pieces, mainstream clothing and quirky vintage finds to create her personal look.

'Have nothing in your homes
that you do not know to be useful
and believe to be beautiful.'

– William Morris

The Mix Makes all the Difference

What works for fashion, works in your interior as well. Mix and match price points, styles, colours, textures, new and old, to achieve stunning results and save your wallet as well. Some people are born mixers, they always seem to get it right, no matter what they buy, it seems to work in their interior. Believe me, everyone can learn this skill. There is only one rule to follow: only buy things that mean something to you. Travel souvenirs are a great example. Integrate them in your home and you will always be reminded of a wonderful holiday you spent. The best results are sometimes achieved because you have to work to a budget: you have already invested in your favourite designer chairs, so now you need to find creative ways to complement your interior. Check out (warehouse) sales, discontinued line reductions, second-hand shops and antique and vintage dealers. Research online shops specialising in furniture for small spaces.

Once you have established your decorating essentials and made your wish list (DREAM ROOM), think about creative ways to add the icing on the cake. Make a deal with yourself: 'I am going to invest in two stunning chairs, and find an inexpensive mainstream lounge to combine with them.' Do this in each room. And be courageous and confident that you can mix and match. There are no real rules, this is a very intuitive and personal game. But, rest assured, that every piece of furniture or décor that means something to you, and therefore has a reason for being in the mix, will work.

This method will take longer than buying everything from one place (and look), but believe me it is much more fun and you will create a very individual and stylish outcome: your home!

Don't be frustrated because you think you will never be able to afford your dream home. The opposite is the case: imagine your dream home and then let it go! Famous American interior designer Elsie de Wolfe wrote in 1913 in her book *The House in Good Taste:* 'There was never a house so bad that it could not be made over into something worthwhile. We shall all be very much happier when you learn how to transform the things you have into a semblance of our ideal.' The goal is to create a home that reflects your personality, a home that makes you happy and where you can relax and re-energise.

'We are shaped and fashioned by what we love.'

– Johann Wolfgang von Goethe

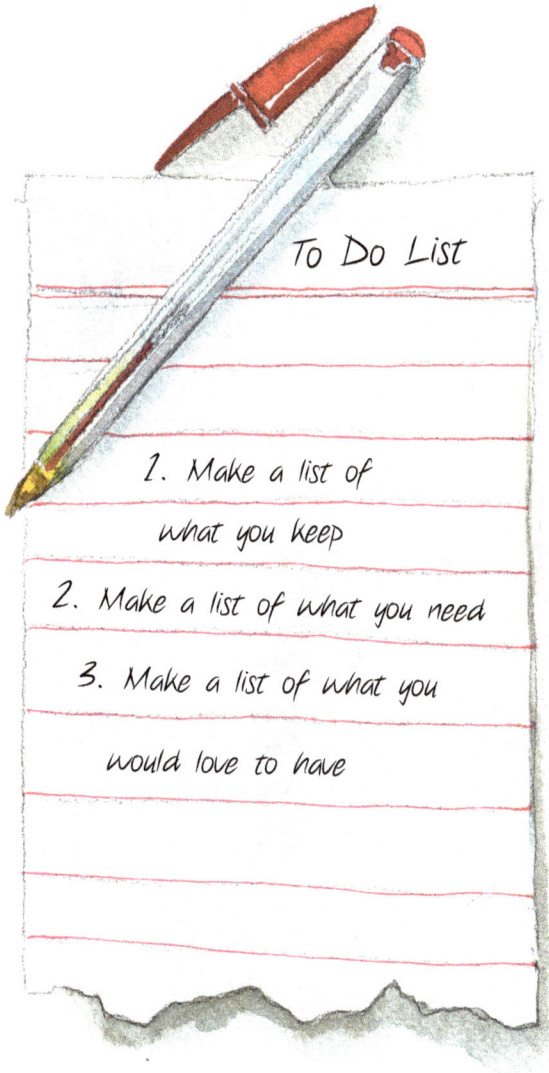

To Do List

1. Make a list of
   what you keep

2. Make a list of what you need

3. Make a list of what you
   would love to have

Dream Notes

My Dream Dining/Living Area

My style of entertaining:

The focal point is:

My dining table should look like:

My dining table should seat:

I want the living area to be:

I would love to have:

My Dream Bedroom

I want the master bedroom to be:

A must have is:

The focal point is:

I would love to have:

My Dream Bathroom

I want the bathroom to be:

A must have is:

The focal point is:

The atmosphere I would like to achieve is:

I would love to have:

My Dream Study/Work Space

I want the study to be:

A must have is:

The focal point is:

I would love to have:

Toolbox

- ☐ Progress Chart
- ☐ Budget Checklist
- ☐ Project Folder Checklist
- ☐ Project Folder Title
- ☐ Worksheet – Inventory
- ☐ Worksheet – Decorating Essentials
- ☐ Worksheet – Dream Home
- ☐ Tips & Tricks – De-clutter Your Paperwork
- ☐ Tips & Tricks – De-clutter Your Linen Cupboard
- ☐ Tips & Tricks – How to Fold a Fitted Sheet
- ☐ Tips & Tricks – De-clutter Your Kitchen
- ☐ Tips & Tricks – De-clutter Your Wardrobe

Notes

Step 2: Find Your Personal Decorating Style

Scenario

Belinda and Tom downsized five years ago to a semi on Sydney's North Shore. They have de-cluttered lots of their 'stuff' and passed on things to family, friends, and charities; they also sold some of their possessions. Belinda only kept what she loved most. They managed to simplify their life and prepare their retirement. They were able to free up their minds to spark their creativity for things they always wanted to do. They feel that their stuff doesn't own them any longer. They can enjoy their beloved pieces much better without all the clutter around. They are now ready to downsize again to an apartment in the same area where they currently live. They are excited to start a new chapter of their life and figure out how to decorate the new apartment, especially with regard to incorporating their favourite pieces and creating an exciting new interior. They can't wait to start their new life adventure.

For Belinda and Tom it is time to enhance their personal decorating style. They have de-cluttered and know what they want to take to their new apartment. They are ready to start a new journey – including the decorating of their new space. To be able to create a truly unique and inspiring home it is worth going on a self-discovery journey to find out more about your personal decorating style.

This is one of the most exciting steps when decorating. It allows you to inject your personality into your space. It allows you to be creative and express yourself. All you need is the willingness to dig deep inside yourself and find out what you love and what makes you happy. You have to do the job a designer usually does in the initial consultation. Designers, who are serious about helping you to achieve your desired outcome, should ask a lot of questions and listen to you. They will need to find out how you live, how you use your space and what you want to achieve with your project. They need to gather as much information as possible to be able to help you to achieve your desired outcome.

To make your home unique and inspiring, you need to allocate time to reflect on how you can inject your personality.

Think about your childhood and past life and learn how to be inspired by everything around you. Check out the exercises in this chapter. Be courageous and confident to use the things you love and mix them with new things in a new environment. Don't be afraid to make mistakes. If you don't like what you do, change it. You can always re-paint a wall or move cushions to another room. Your home should be an extension of yourself, of yourself as a child, as an adult, or the person you want to be in the future.

To personalise your home also demands patience. The creative process can't be forced. Sometimes it takes weeks to get the right

idea or to find the right piece to finish off your interior. Other times the solution for a problem or challenge you might have seems to come to you easily and things fall into place. I experience this when painting. I have worked on some paintings for months, and others I finished in a couple of hours including the initial idea for the composition.

For Belinda and Tom I would recommend putting their creative thinking hat on and starting to explore how they can begin decorating from the heart.

You are downsizing and looking to create an inspiring and stylish home. In order to achieve this, you need to find your personal decorating style. I believe that everybody has a certain decorating style, some people just don't know how to name it. Don't be confused if you like a mix of different styles and things. Perhaps you are like me and like an eclectic mix of industrial furniture with sleek contemporary pieces and Art Deco-style furniture and décor. This may seem a bit all over the place, but it is much more personal than a look from a catalogue or a famous designer people pay a lot of money for. You don't have to find one single word for it, gather your inspirations and tear sheets from magazines (read more about tear sheets on page 65, and find words to describe it.

If you are not sure what you like, or not confident enough to buy the pieces you really love, the following exercises are for you. Even if you think, 'that sounds silly' or 'it is too much effort', trust me and try it. Step out of your comfort zone and choose a different path! This is something I learned in my yoga classes: only by stepping out of our comfort zone are we able to experience something new and make room for new things to happen. If you follow my advice you will decorate your new home with ease, create a personal and stylish interior and eventually refine your apartment lifestyle.

I will show you three proven methods to find or enhance your personal decorating style.

Now that you have de-cluttered, tidied up and created your lists of what you want and need, it is time to go on a self-discovery journey. This is the first step in creating your personal decorating style. As American fashion icon Iris Apfel says: you have to learn who you are first. So put your thinking hat on and reflect what you love in life. Go on a self-discovery journey! Depending on your personality, choose one of the following three methods, or try them all. They are fun, believe me!

1. Create the Story of Who You Are

An interesting way to find out more about yourself is to create a story of who you are. The inspiration for this exercise comes from Stephen Denning, author of the book *The Leader's Guide to Storytelling*. I have done this exercise myself and found it quite astonishing. What I am passionate about now clearly relates back to my childhood. If it works for me, it will work for you too. You only need a pen and paper and to schedule a time to do it.

Divide your piece of paper into three sections. Draw a dot in the middle section and title this section: 'Where I am now'. Then draw a cross in the first section and name this section: 'Where I have come from'. The third section represents the future. Draw a circle and name it: 'Where I am heading'. In this section you write your life goal or any thoughts you connect to your future. You could answer the question: 'What do I want to achieve in the future'? The next step is to draw a line from the cross through the dot to the circle. This line represents the journey of your life. I have prepared a worksheet for you ready to download from the toolbox on www.downsizewithstyle.com.

Now it is time to go back to your childhood. Think about a one-minute story about one of these topics. Select one of the following questions:

* What was a favourite place when you were young and what made it special to you?

* How did you manage to overcome an obstacle when you were young?

* Describe an incident with a person you admired or who influenced you

* What was the most significant thing that happened to you in your childhood?

Once you have chosen your story, give it a name. Then review it for the following points:

* Does your story reflect the person you are today?
* Are your personal values reflected in your story?
* Does your story distinguish you from other people?
* Is your story consistent? Does it reflect the way you lead your life now?

The next step is to tell your story to your friends and see how it evolves. You can repeat this process with different subjects until you get a portfolio of stories, which represents who you are.

2. Make Pinterest Your Best Friend

Use your computer to research what you love. A fantastic tool for inspiration and creativity is the online pin board Pinterest (www. pinterest.com). You can sign up for free and start pinning what inspires you. Choose categories that interest you and you will see images that other people pinned in this category. You can re-pin them on your own boards.

Create boards for

* Your favourite colour(s)
* Your favourite furniture pieces
* Things you love
* Places you love to hang around
* Your favourite place to relax

* Your favourite place to travel
* Your perfect weekend
* Your favourite shops
* Your hobby
* Your favourite movies
* Your favourite books
* Your favourite magazines
* Your favourite artists

For example, if you love shells and driftwood, and the beach is your favourite place to relax, type these words in the search field and create your own 'Beach Style' board with the images that speak to you. Or you could start creating colour boards for your favourite colours. Then create a board for your new apartment lifestyle and pin all your inspirations to this board. These mood boards will additionally be a great starting point for any interior decorator, should you decide to seek professional help.

Try it, but be careful, it can be addictive! I always need to set myself a time when browsing Pinterest, because I just can't get enough from all the gorgeous pictures people have pinned worldwide. I love creating themed boards and use them frequently as inspiration for myself or to show my clients what they can achieve in a specific room or with a certain colour scheme. And, because a picture is worth a 1000 words, it will become crystal clear what you like, once you have sorted all your inspirations to different boards. Additionally, you will get a pretty good idea what your new space is going to look like.

If you pin a picture from the web always credit (reference) the website and photographer, respecting their copyright.

3. Become an Explorer of the World

If you are more of an outdoor type, you may prefer the following exercise. A fun way of finding your own style is departing on a world discovery tour. The good thing is you don't have to travel far and wide. Start in your home, your street, your suburb. Go for a walk and explore the world around you.

Inspiration can be found everywhere: nature, architecture, buildings, shops, exhibitions, museums, art, events, markets.

If you see something you like, take a picture or make a note why you like it. For example, you are going for a walk and spot a gorgeous flower, stop and take a picture. If you are in the city and a building catches your eye, take a picture of the whole building or the particular feature that made you stop. You can even find inspiration while you are shopping. I am always attracted to interesting and quirky window displays. As most big shops have their in-store visual merchandising team, you can learn a lot about how to create an interesting display in your own home by watching what professional product stylists have implemented in a shop window.

Take a weekend to visit an exhibition or art gallery for inspiration. Think about why you like a certain painting, sculpture or photography. Do something different and enrol in an art class to re-activate your creativity – even if you believe you are the most uncreative person on the planet! You will be surprised what you discover when stepping out of your comfort zone!

Always carry a little notebook and a camera (or your smart phone) with you to capture and write down what inspires you. Do this on a consistent basis and you will see a pattern emerge regarding the colours, textures and styles you like.

The most important thing is to keep your eyes open and your mind excited! Discover and appreciate the beauty that lies within everything that surrounds you.

Another fantastic source of inspiration is magazines and books. Despite the triumph of the internet and mobile reading devices, I could never, ever live without my printed books and magazines.

'Everyone is an artist.'

– Joseph Beuys

I am totally addicted to interior design magazines and read them on a regular basis. But I am not suggesting interior design magazines only. Depending on your interests, visit a good newsagent and flick through some special interest magazines that speak to you. Start a collection of tear sheets from these magazines. Do this for four to eight weeks and you will again see a pattern emerge. Compare it to the findings from your pictures and the notes you took.

Then, there are the coffee table books, of course! I can spend hours looking at my coffee table books, feeling the beautiful paper and looking at the pictures. And I enjoy seeing them sitting on the shelf, or beautifully decorating a side table. I love my collection of these books and I keep adding more and more. I own books about colour, interior decorating, interior design, art, travel, history, photography, theatre and more.

Book storage is a major topic for apartment downsizers but, probably, like me, you have a large collection of books you can't part with. The good news is: you don't have to get rid of all your books. Choose your favourite ones and use them as design elements. Books, apart from flowers, make a home personal and have the most impact in interior styling. And, there is nothing more interesting than a beautifully curated bookshelf. You can learn a lot about the homeowner by looking at his or her book collection – or looking through it!

'Keep your eyes open and
your mind excited.
Through passion and participation
things will open to you
and opportunities arise.'

– Eve Bartolo

One of my favourite books, which I spotted in a museum shop, is called: *How to be an Explorer of the World* by Keri Smith. On the back it says: 'At any given moment, no matter where you are, there are hundreds of things around you that are interesting and worth documenting.' I kept reading the book in the store and ended up buying it, as it really made me think about the little things around us, and how important it is to appreciate them all.

Inspirational Movies for Interior Decorators

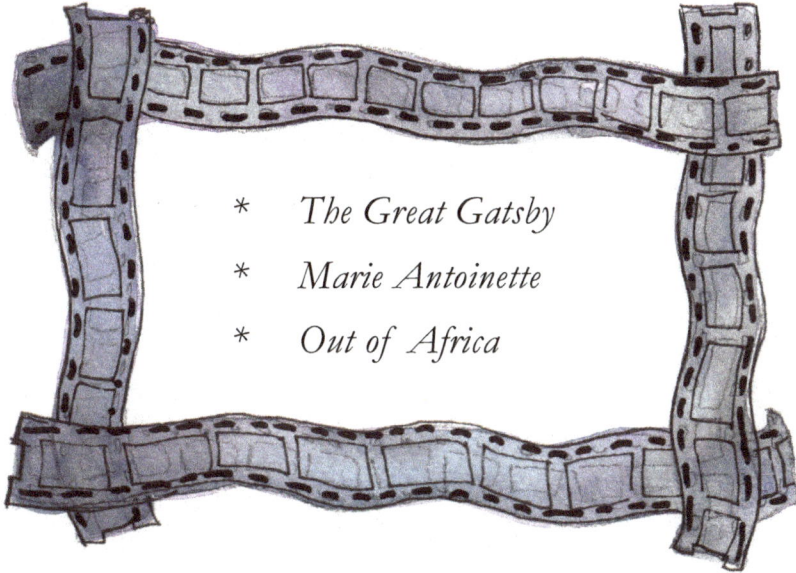

* *The Great Gatsby*
* *Marie Antoinette*
* *Out of Africa*

When I first saw The Great Gatsby I was completely overwhelmed by the beauty of the Art Deco interiors and fashion. I instantly decided to buy this movie on DVD and watch it again – firstly, because I absolutely love the Art Deco period and secondly, to be able to stop the movie where I wanted to immerse myself in the most beautiful interiors ever! This movie is a great example of how the little details make all the difference in an interior. Do you remember the Art Deco teapot and cups in the scene when Gatsby met Daisy for the first time in his neighbour's cottage? Just divine! One of my favourite stylists, Megan Morton, even recommends turning off the sound when watching a movie the second time to be able to fully concentrate on the interiors.

To Do List

1. Buy a gorgeous notebook

2. Choose one of the three methods to find your personal decorating style

3. Schedule a time and go for it!

4. Collect your findings (in your physical project folder or online)

Toolbox

☐   Worksheet – Self Discovery

☐   Worksheet – Your Story

What do i want?

DREAM BIG, BE CREATIVE, MIX & MATCH

Step 3: Visualise Your Ideas

Scenario

Jess, 45, has gone through a divorce and is going to move into a 2-bedroom apartment, which she has bought off the plan. The apartment will be finished in a couple of months. Apart from a contemporary white kitchen and a neutral coloured bathroom, it will be empty. Jess has a few inherited antique furniture pieces and a contemporary lounge that she would like to incorporate into her new home. She is looking forward to decorating her apartment with the things she loves and add some new items. Flicking through interior design magazines she has recently found some great ideas for colour schemes for her living area. She also loves art and has two colourful canvasses she would love to display as well.

Jess already has some ideas for her new apartment that she would like to become reality. This is the perfect time for a mood board to visualise her ideas and get a clearer picture about the look and feel of the space she is working on.

To get started I recommend purchasing a foam core board or use a pin board you might already have. Take your tear sheets and inspirations from magazines and pin them on your board. Add pictures of your favourite furniture pieces you would like to incorporate. Include little objects that speak to you or remind you of a great place or holiday. These objects might be ribbons, buttons, shells, scrap paper, tags, tickets, photographs or travel souvenirs. Finalise your board with colour and fabric swatches. In Jess's case, I recommend including a picture of her artworks, which can function as the starting point for her interior colour scheme.

Keep working on your mood board until it feels right for you. The good thing with these boards is that you can play around, add, remove and re-pin as you go. There is no right or wrong, it is all about how you can bring your heart and soul into your new space. You will see your interior come alive on your board.

Once Jess is ready to move in, she can test her mood board onsite and see how her colour and decorating ideas work in the new space. Her mood board will function as an inspiration board in the new apartment. She can even display it in her living area and use it as guideline to complete her interior.

I always recommend taking your time when decorating a new space. Sometimes you need to live there for a few months to find out what to change or what is missing.

This chapter is all about how to visualise your ideas, thoughts and findings. This is an important step in the whole process of creating your new home – especially if you are not sure that your ideas will work or not yet confident enough to put your interior together.

Visualising and translating your ideas on a mood board will

*   spark your creativity
*   help you stay organised and in control of your project
*   define your colour scheme
*   paint a clear picture of the overall look and feel of your space
*   improve your skills as interior decorator.

I am going to show you step-by-step how to develop a mood board and how to translate your ideas into your space. Designers of all genres use this method to visualise their design concepts to their clients. If you search Wikipedia you find the following explanation: 'A **mood board** is a type of poster design that may consist of images, text, and samples of objects in a composition of the choice of the mood board creator.'

Collect, Curate, Create

Now, let's go into the details of how to start your mood board. Firstly, you will need your inspiration collection. Go through your collected objects, colour samples, fabric swatches, tear sheets and choose everything that works for you in the specific room you are working on. If you found that you love French Provincial style, for example, add elements and objects to your board that translate this mood to your space.

You can use a piece of foam core or presentation board (available in art shops) or an old picture frame. Pin, glue or tape your objects on your board. Be eclectic and choose objects from different sources. Bring in some quirky elements, something unexpected! Be a curator of your inspirations!

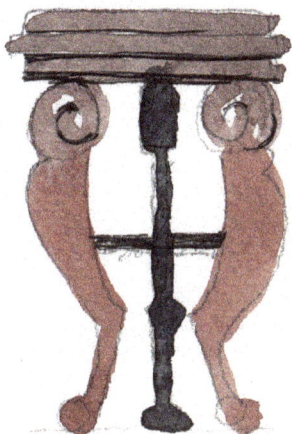

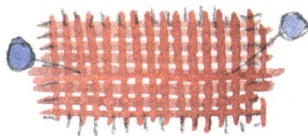

Alternatively, you can create your mood board on a large tray or in a box, if you don't have the space to hang it on the wall. The most important thing is that you find a pattern from all your inspirational pieces and combine your overall style with the feeling you want to convey. Your board should translate the mood and atmosphere you want to achieve in your space.

'Creativity takes courage.'

– Henri Matisse

A large (A3 format) style journal is another way to gather your inspirations.

This is very helpful if you go browsing stores or markets as you then have with you a reference to show what you want, and to check that your new purchases and finds work with what you already have.

The next step is to position the mood board in the room you want to decorate and test it in situ. Leave it there for a few days and watch how colours and textures and the overall look work in the room at different times of the day. Test some elements from the board in your room. For example, tape a large colour swatch on your wall to see how the colour will transform the room. Organise a fabric sample and place it over the arm of a chair to get an idea of how this fabric would look in your interior.

Take your time to add or remove items and tweak the overall

look and feel. After a few days you have a solid foundation to decide to either go ahead with this look or to rethink and create something new.

You probably think that this sounds all very time consuming and requires a lot of effort. Well, haste makes waste, and while a good mood board may take quite a bit of your time, it is the basis for your new home. The more time you allocate to this (fun) task, the better your outcome will be. So be patient: it is the same as with yoga, the journey is the reward.

And it will save you a lot of time as well! During my time as sales consultant in a furniture store, I talked to a lot of customers who had no clear idea what they wanted and what they were looking for. They arrived in the store already frustrated and told me that they had been looking for several months and could not find anything that they liked. They kept turning in circles. To avoid this, you have to strategise your project, work to a plan, and be clear what you want before you start shopping.

Toolbox

☐   Checklist – Mood Board

Downsize with Style

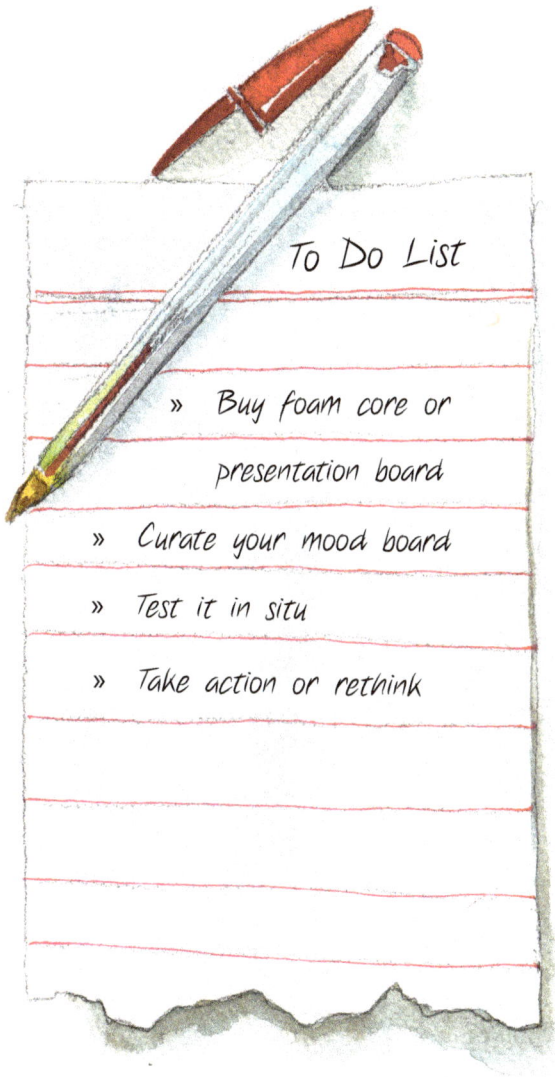

To Do List

» Buy foam core or
  presentation board

» Curate your mood board

» Test it in situ

» Take action or rethink

Step 4: Layout Your Space

Scenario

John and Jenny are in their fifties and starting to consider the idea of downsizing. They realise that they will not need as much furniture or as many accessories as in their current home, but they have not considered the scale of their pieces in proportion to the new, smaller home. They are not sure if their furniture will fit in a smaller space or how big the space needs to be to make it work. They keep putting off the decision to downsize, because it is too daunting.

To make crystal clear what will fit in a smaller home, you need to layout your space. Measure the furniture pieces you would like to take with you. If you already have an apartment in mind you would like to buy, take the scale of your floor plan and draw your furniture to the same scale. All you need is a piece of paper and

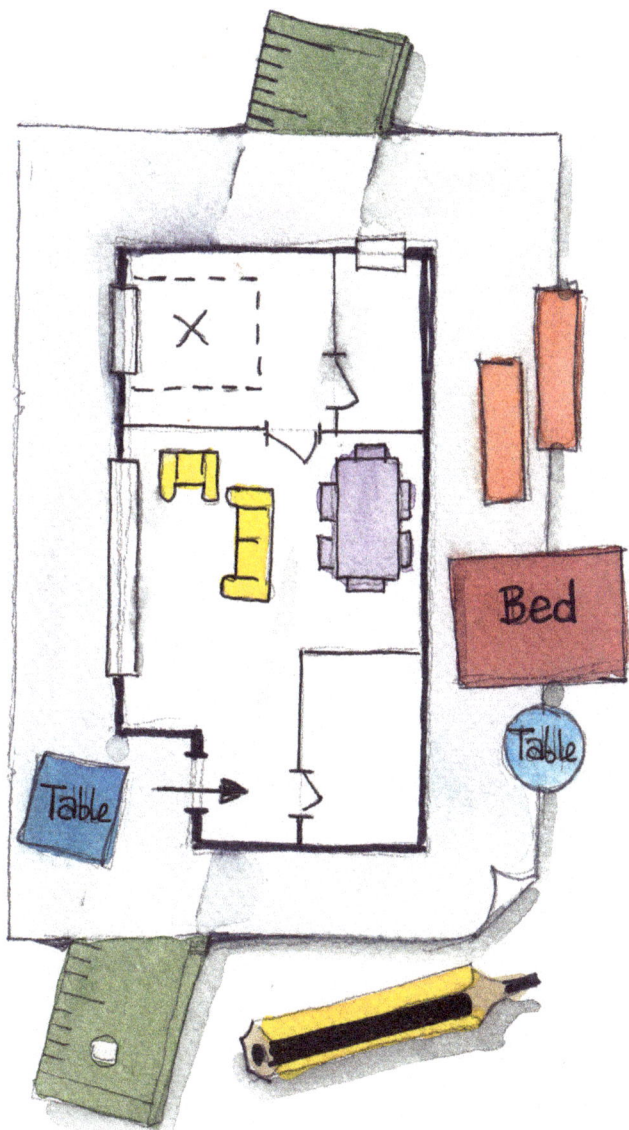

Bed

Table

Table

✕

a scale ruler. Then cut out the shapes of your furniture and place them on your floor plan. Move them around to create different looks and see if they will fit. If it does look too big on the paper, it won't work in the apartment.

If you have not yet decided on a new space, work with your furniture shapes and calculate how big a new home would need to be to fit your pieces. This gives you an indication of what to look for when researching housing options.

A general rule of thumb is that smaller pieces are much easier to move around and, with some creativity, can be used for different purposes. Consider this when buying new furniture while you are still in your family home.

It is also a wonderful opportunity to redecorate your new space and create a new look combining a couple of feature pieces from your family home with some new pieces. There is a wide range of versatile and stylish furniture available that suits an apartment lifestyle.

You have come a long way now and can be proud of your achievements. You have mastered the unpopular task of de-cluttering and have decided what to take to your new home. You also went on a self-discovery journey and immersed yourself in the creative process of visualisation. Once you have decided on the look and feel of your room, it is time to layout the space.

As you most probably are moving to a smaller space than your family home, you may find it hard to visualise how your furniture will fit and how you can make a small space look larger. By drawing up your rooms you will get a better idea of the size and proportion and of the overall look of your new home.

This may sound a bit scary, especially if you are not very confident in drawing. But, trust me, it is not that hard and you will see immediately if your interior will work, or if you need to rethink your furniture placement.

All you need is a scale ruler and grid paper. Draw the floor plan of your apartment to a chosen scale. Then measure your tables, chairs, lounges, sideboard, console, etc. and draw each piece to the same scale. Cut the pieces out. Now you can place them on your floor plan and move them around to find the best layout for your apartment.

More tech-savvy readers can search for online floor planning websites. Some programs are free of charge; some require a subscription or payment as you go. The advantage is that you can view your floor plans in 2D and 3D. The downside is that you will need to invest extra time to learn how to use them. I recommend the old pencil and paper method, because it is quick and you don't need your computer.

Think Like a Designer

Once you have completed this step, it is time to think like a designer. To be able to do this, it is handy to understand the elements and principles of design. They are the basis for all design work and will help you create impact in your hozme.

I like to use the analogy of baking a cake. Think about the ingredients you need for your cake – these are the elements of design. Then imagine the process of making the cake, what do you do first, what comes next etc. These are the principles of design.

Elements of design are:

Line, direction, shape, size/proportion, colour, tone and texture

Principles of design are:

Harmony, contrast, dominance, balance, rhythm, unity and repetition

Combining elements and principles of design you can create interesting interiors that are balanced and calming or colourful and stimulating. The world is your oyster. For example, if you use bold colours for your walls and décor, offset with neutral furniture, you create a contrast and dominance of colour. If your interior is all white with little tonal variation, but lots of different textures, your interior is characterised by a harmony in tone and dominance in texture. Flick through some interior design magazines and look at interiors you like with the elements and principles of design in mind. This is an interesting exercise and helps you understand why you like a certain interior. Then apply these principles in your own home.

Ideas for Apartment Room Layouts

In this chapter I am going to give you some general tips on (clever) room layouts as well as cover some key challenges for downsizers: how to make a small space look larger and how to optimise storage in a smaller space.

Small spaces require clever space management and room layouts. Every square metre needs to be used. Another important point to consider is the traffic flow through your apartment. This advice I have given to homeowners who are preparing their home for

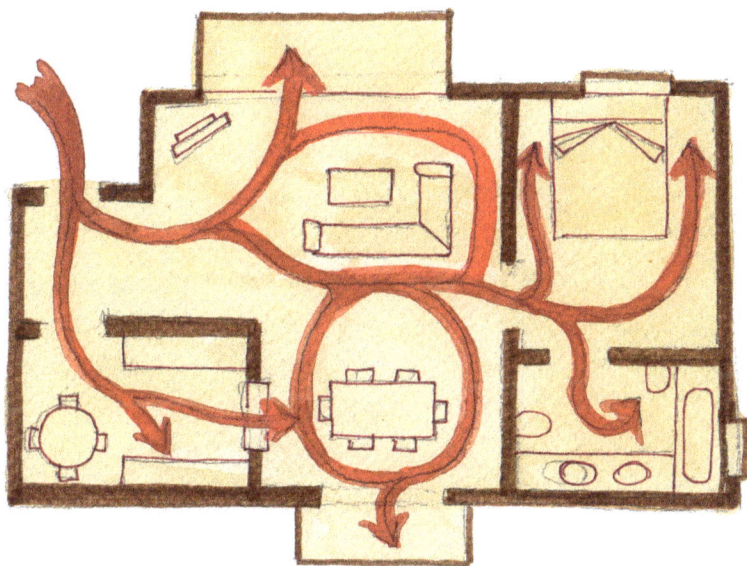

sale. As they expect lots of people walking through their property, they need to provide wide access on the major routes through their house. Plan your home's circulation and your space will work automatically. Take your floor plan and draw lines on it for the major routes through your apartment. These routes need maximum width, as more people will use them. Make sure that your furniture placement allows for optimised traffic flow and circulation. Don't block traffic routes with furniture pieces so that people have to walk around them. For less congested routes, provide narrower access.

Always direct your furniture towards the best features of your apartment. For example, if you have stunning water views from your living area, position your dining table so that everyone can enjoy the view without having to turn their heads. Position your lounge in a way to be able to enjoy the view and watch TV.

Kitchen

Kitchens are the centre and backbone of the house where we spend a lot of time during the day. Kitchens are being transformed more and more into socialising and entertaining spaces – even entertaining our guests happens in the kitchen. This is the number one reason to invest in this space.

When looking to buy an apartment to downsize, make sure that there are high quality appliances and materials used in the kitchen. As a general rule of thumb, invest in everything you touch or work with on a daily basis: the cook top, range hood, oven, fridge and your bench top. These are the kitchen essentials, everything else is decoration.

I know that kitchen islands are very popular in Australia but, to be honest, I am not a big fan of these benches. This is simply because they never look in real life as they look in the real estate brochures. Living in, and using your kitchen, means there will always be clutter of some form visible on the bench. And if your sink is in the middle of the bench it will be even worse. Think of dirty dishes piled up during your dinner party. I am a fan of what I call half-open kitchen spaces. This can be achieved by adding a bar height bench to the side of your kitchen that faces the dining and living area. Your kitchen will still open, the bar is a great place to entertain and you can hide all your stuff behind it.

A few years ago I heard a New Zealand kitchen designer talk about a trend towards organic-shaped benches and kitchen islands with different height counters. If you browse kitchen websites or brochures you can definitely see this happening. Another huge trend is the kitchen with no handles, to create a streamlined and sleek look. Appliances can be recessed in the wall. Especially if you have a small space where kitchen and living areas are combined, this solution looks tidy and neat and makes the space look larger. The kitchen becomes an integrated furniture piece.

Dining and Living

Most probably you will have an open-plan kitchen, dining and living area in your new apartment. This is the centre of your home and the place where you entertain your family and friends. You will spend most the time in the day in this space. Therefore, comfort and quality should be the number one thing to look for.

Invest in a great dining table and comfortable chairs. Don't go for chairs that only look good. Sit in them! The most important thing is that they are comfortable for your family and guests, and that you can spend hours sitting in them. Make sure that you have a least an 80 cm space behind the dining chairs enabling everyone to sit comfortably around the table for socialising. If you plan to have a round dining table make sure you measure your space exactly, as a round table will need more space than a rectangular one with the same number of chairs.

Consider a glass table or a table with a light base to make the space look larger. If you have enough space, a table with extendable leaves is a stylish option. This will allow you to optimise space when you are alone and extend your table to spend precious time with your favourite people.

The dining room is also a great area for decorating and displaying your favourite pieces or collections. Be creative and look for a less expensive option here: an antique or retro display cabinet from an auction centre might do the trick. Another option could be a shelf as a room divider. Display your heirlooms and treasures there and instantly inject your personality into your space. Place your favourite piece of art in this space. Create a conversation starter for your guests.

With open-plan areas, the secret is to treat each area as an island and define it through colour, lighting or an area rug. There are some clever furniture pieces available (some with castors to easily move them around), which act as bar table, storage device and room divider at the same time.

If you take the word living area literally, it means a space to live in. This space should be comfortable in the first place, and an inviting and inspiring space as well, as this is the centre for communication and the gathering of family and friends. Think about how you use your room: is it merely for communicating with your partner, family and friends, or do you also watch TV in this area? According to your preferences, design and set up the room. Decorate around your focal point. This can be an architectural feature like a fireplace with a mantel, for example. I will give you some tips on how to decorate a mantel in Step 5.

A small space does not necessarily look larger if all your furniture is pushed to the walls. Move your lounge and chairs away from the walls and experience how different this feels when you use this space.

Another way to create spaciousness is to use the same colour throughout your entrance, kitchen, living and dining area.

Use smaller furniture pieces, which are versatile and easy to move around. Think of a couple of single chairs with legs instead of a 2-seater lounge, two to four sleek side tables instead of one bulky coffee table, or a set of four square ottomans that can be used separately to sit on, or as footstools, or be joined together with a tray on top as a coffee table. Play with different heights for your side and coffee tables and use a pouf or ottoman to create interesting seating areas. Additionally, you can add colour and texture with these pieces. Avoid massive modular lounges or heavy chairs and tables without legs. They are hard to move and look very bulky in a small space.

If you love your book collection, consider a floor to ceiling bookshelf. Here, you have the chance to create a real focal point by not only displaying your books, but also curating interesting objects, sculptures or other collectibles you might have (see Step 5 for how to decorate a bookshelf).

'It is sad when you feel uncomfortable in a beautiful chair.'

– BoConcept Catalogue 2013

The TV is most probably the biggest enemy of an interior stylist. Unfortunately, digital TVs get bigger and bigger and use up a lot of space that could be used for styling and decorating. If you have your TV in your living room, and don't want it to be the focal point, consider adequate storage or a built-in solution to hide it away when not used. As most TV screens are black, you have to be aware of this massive black surface in your space. If you love black and white and use these colours in your space, it will blend in. But in any other colour scheme, the black TV screen will stand out and you will have to work around it. One option is to place the screen on a wall. This will automatically make it the focal point in the room. By surrounding your flat screen with artworks or other interesting objects you can create a gallery wall and integrate the screen in a larger arrangement. Be aware of the proportions of your screen and the surrounding pieces. Work with similar sizes to create a unified look (refer to the elements and principles of design).

'There was never a house so bad that it could not be made over into something worthwhile. We shall all be very much happier when you learn how to transform the things you have into a semblance of our ideal.'

– Elsie de Wolfe, 1913

Bedroom

Your bedroom is a great place to express yourself! It should be your sanctuary and more than comfortable! It is your place to relax and chill out. So make it as personal and intimate as you like. Neutral colours or pastels in blue, green and grey create a calming atmosphere and suit both women and men. To add a splash of your favourite colour use it as accent in cushions, decorative objects or flowers.

The focal point in a bedroom is usually the bed. You spend a third of your life in bed, so invest in a quality mattress first of all! You know how vital it is in today's hectic world to rest and have a good night's sleep. Then think about how much storage you need. Consider under-bed storage, an ottoman with storage option or a built-in bookshelf around the bed. Going for this option you can use one compartment of the shelf as a bedside table and a clamp lamp as a reading light. Reading lights also look very stylish when mounted on the wall behind the bed or hung from the ceiling above the bed. With this solution, however, you have to keep in mind that rearranging the furniture will involve changing the position of the pendants as well. Small baskets are great organisers for all the little pieces you keep in your bedroom and can be placed in the shelf. If you can do without bedside tables this will save you space and make your bedroom look larger.

Another option to make a statement in the bedroom is to use the wall behind the bed as a blank canvas and decorate it with either a gorgeous bed head, wallpaper (very popular and millions of patterns and styles to choose from!) or a couple of shelves above the bed to display art, family photos and treasured objects.

If you can't do without bedside tables, look for a slim shape with legs or a transparent perspex cube which can be used to store books and magazines inside it. Alternatively, use a small stool or a stack of books as a table. Be creative and unique in your private space!

For additional storage, a bench at the end of the bed is a stylish (think of a gorgeous fabric!) and practical solution. If the size of your bedroom allows it, create a cosy reading corner with an occasional chair and a little side table.

For wardrobes and linen closets, sliding doors are a great option, as they do not hinder furniture placement.

Depending on the aspect of your bedroom choose the right window coverings. Do you need light-blocking drapery to keep out the sun or only a decorative sheer? Have a decorative cushion made in the same fabric as your curtains to link your room.

If you have a contemporary-style apartment consider adjustable external venetian blinds. Especially for north and west facing rooms they are very efficient in keeping out the heat and sun. And if not completely closed, you can still look through and enjoy the view.

Bathroom

For bathrooms the same principles apply as for kitchens. Make sure your new apartment has quality products installed for everything you touch and use every day: tap ware, shower, bathtub, toilet, and heated towel rails.

Extended tiles from floor to ceiling will draw up the eye and make the space seem larger. Wall hung vanities, toilets and storage units create a feeling of space by freeing up the floor area. Mirrors and high gloss cabinetry reflects light and will make the bathroom feel airy.

If the size of the bathroom allows it, add a small bench or stool for optional seating.

Guest Room/Study

Assuming that you only have one spare room in your apartment, make the most out of it! Think about how you would like to use this room and which furniture pieces are the essentials to make that happen (refer to your lists from Step 1). Furniture, which is versatile and flexible, will make all the difference in this room!

As guest rooms are only used temporarily, they are a stylist's heaven! Use this space as your playground for decorating and trying new things. Surprise your guests with small things like fluffy towels on the bed, scented candles or a bunch of flowers on the bedside table. Probably not the biggest room in your apartment, manipulate this space with the clever use of colour. Use lighter tones for walls and ceiling. Add a rug in the same tonal level. Then bring in your individual style with colourful cushions, throws and accessories. To change the look, replace the accessories and re-decorate.

Optimise this space by furnishing and decorating it as two rooms: guest room and study. The secret is to source furniture that is versatile and can be used for different purposes. For example, use a comfortable sofa bed, which functions as cosy lounge in your study and as bed for your guests. Place a nest of tables next to the sofa bed and add an occasional chair as a seating option for your guests. Use a small desk (check out trestle tables!) with a comfortable chair for your work, and as additional table for your guests. Once they arrive, place a small mirror on the desk to transform it into a dressing table. Keep it free of clutter, and it will work as occasional table for your visitors. Use an open shelf with stylish storage boxes to organise your office space and store books and magazines. Another versatile piece and great (office) storage unit is a chest of drawers. Leave the first two drawers empty for your guests' belongings. Alternatively, use a storage cabinet with sliding doors. Be creative with your wall space and place coloured wall hooks in an interesting pattern to create an eye-catching display and clothes hook for your guests.

This is just one example of how you can optimise the use of one space with clever furniture and decorating ideas. It is just a matter of taking the time to source the right pieces. And, as I already mentioned, you don't have to do everything yourself. Consider assistance from an interior decorator to find the right pieces for your space.

Stylists' Tips & Tricks

How to Make a Small Space Look Larger

1. Manipulate a space through colour
2. Implement intelligent design
3. Source clever furniture
4. Focus on the floor
5. Decorate like a pro

1. Manipulate a Space Through Colour

Colour is the most powerful tool when it comes to non-verbal communication. It is the design element that can change a space immediately. A different colour on the walls can completely change the atmosphere of a space. Colour brings individuality to a space and it is one of the most useful tools to master when decorating.

Visit a hardware store or paint shop to dive into the realm of colour. Pick colours that instantly speak to you. See if you can match your favourite colours to colours you have found in nature or during your discovery tours. When choosing a colour for your home, it is important to think about the mood and atmosphere you would like to achieve in a space. Colour can stimulate us or evoke feelings of calmness and serenity. Colours remind us of past events in our childhood or great holidays we spent with our family.

Colour Theory

A colour is defined by three characteristics: the hue or name of the colour, the intensity or dullness, and the tonal value (compared to its equal grey on a 9-step grey scale from black to white). Each colour also has a consistent attribute called its light reflectance value (LRV) that indicates how light or dark a colour will feel on a wall. The LRV is measured on a scale from 0 to 100 percent, a 50 percent LRV would correspond to a mid-tone on the grey scale and gives you some orientation when choosing your paint colours.

Darker tones with a LRV of 40 percent and under will absorb more light and make the room appear smaller. If you want to create a cosy atmosphere in a small space, go for darker colours. Colours with a LRV higher than 50 percent will be lighter once on the wall and therefore reflect more light back into the room. If you look through the Dulux paint chips or Colour Atlas you will find many colours in full, half and quarter strengths. If you like very light tones of yellow, green or pink, double check the LRV for quarter strengths tones. The LRV can easily go over 80 percent. If you consider painting a whole wall in one of those colours in a room with a lot of natural sunlight you could end up needing your sunglasses when using the room in summer.

The same applies to whites. North and west facing rooms with lots of natural light will be hard to live with when painted in pure whites with a LRV over 90 percent.

Colour not only manipulates the proportions of a room, it also creates a certain mood and atmosphere. Depending on the size and shape of your room and the height of your ceilings, there are different methods to manipulate a room through the way you apply your paint colour.

To make a small space look larger, use light tones of your chosen colour on all surfaces: floor, walls, ceiling. This ensures that the most light possible will be reflected. If your apartment has a dark floor, work with area rugs in light tones of your chosen colour scheme.

Cool colours in light tones recede, which means, that a wall painted in a cool colour will seem further away and make the space look larger. Conversely, if you paint your walls in warm colours and darker tones, it will advance and make the space look smaller.

To raise a ceiling, use a colour that is a lighter tone than the wall colour and paint the walls right up to the ceiling.

To widen a corridor, use light tones of your chosen colour on all surfaces to maximise the light reflection and make the space less confining.

Conversely, if you want to shorten a long hallway or a long

narrow room, paint the end wall in a warm colour and a darker tone to make it advance. To change the proportions in a long corridor or long narrow room, use darker tones on the floor and ceiling. This will make the space appear lower and wider.

What applies to paint colours is also valid for colours in decoration. An all white or neutral interior can be brought to life with the colours you choose for decorative items like rugs, cushions, throws, art, accessories and flowers. Step 5 will cover this in detail.

2. Implement Intelligent Design

Good design will always add value to your apartment. Depending on your needs, look for intelligent design solutions for your home. Think of storage wall units in your living area to hide your TV when not in use. This is my favourite solution to not let the big black screen take over the living area and be automatically the focal point.

Design your dining area with stylish tables that come in different sizes, shapes and colours. Use an extension table as a flexible solution for you and your guests.

Research wall-hung display and storage units. Everything mounted on the wall will make your floor space larger. Wall hung units can be used in living areas, bedrooms and bathrooms.

Sideboards are elegant, functional and great for storage in any room. Hide your stuff in drawers and behind doors and create eye-catching vignettes with your favourite items on top.

Look for furniture companies specialising on apartment furniture. You will find lots of ideas for clever and versatile pieces you may not have thought of.

3. Source Clever Furniture

Building up a database of suppliers over the past three years, I have come across many companies who offer very stylish and yet practical furniture for small spaces. The trick is to find a versatile piece that can be used for different purposes. Look for furniture that can be used as a standalone piece, or be used in combination with other pieces for a different purpose.

The furniture company I worked with in the past offered small square cubes that customers could customise by choosing their own fabric or leather for upholstery. These little cubes could be used as additional seating (in the living or dining area), or as footstools, or arranged as a set of four in a larger square, as coffee table. We offered timber or metal trays in the same size to put on top of the cube. In no time, the customers could re-arrange their living space according to their needs. Additionally, these cubes were stylish decorative pieces allowing the customers to play around with colours, textures and materials to coordinate with their interior.

I also find that Scandinavian designers create wonderful contemporary furniture, with slim lines and lots of customisation options to suit small spaces.

4. Focus on the Floor

A very simple method to make a space look larger is using the same flooring throughout the whole apartment. Especially in open-plan living areas, a single finish from the entrance through the living and dining area will widen the space. This will additionally be enhanced by continuing the chosen finish to the outside entertainment area. There is a huge choice of floor tiles with indoor and outdoor versions available. Timber tiles are also very popular as they add the warmth of the timber look to a space and can be used in the kitchen as well.

5. Decorate like a Pro

In decorating your home you can unleash your creativity! Even if you think you are not creative at all, give it a go and start being inspired by interior designers from all over the world. Research design blogs and follow the ones that speak to you. You will discover that most interior designers love to share their work and inspirations. Borrow the things you like and implement them in your own home, with your modifications. This might be a colour scheme from one of Kevin McCloud's books; a way to layer colour and pattern seen in one of Kit Kemp's famous design hotels; or a coffee table decoration spotted in a furniture store. Be courageous and creative about finding your own decorating style.

Take a few hours to browse bookshops with large design departments. There are design books for every taste and budget. One of my favourite books and creative sources is *Be Your Own Decorator* by Susanna Salk. This book showcases room designs from over 75 acclaimed interior designers worldwide and covers a wide range of styles from traditional to modern. There are lots of details to discover on every single page that you could incorporate in your new home.

'Colours are like musical notes and chords, while colour is a pleasing result of their artistic use in a combined way. So colours are means to an end, while colour is the end itself. The first are tools, while the other is a distinctive harmony in art composed of many lines and shades.'

– Walter Shaw Sparrow

Tips from International Experts

Isn't it great to get advice from people you admire? I asked three interior designers I met (online and offline) in the past couple of years to share their views and inspirations on how to optimise small spaces. Enjoy their take on things and be inspired!

CJ Dellatore is an interior designer and blogger from New York City and an absolute inspiration to me! I found him through blogging and have followed his blog *cjdellatore* ever since. As well as working as a photographer, make-up artist, graphic designer, interior stylist, and printmaker, he worked with Martha Stewart on her magazine and was a textile expert on her television show 'Living'. He then opened his own textile design company, CJ Dellatore Textile. On his blog Carl engages in conversations about design, talks about his design preferences, and generously shares the entire process with his readers.

What is your favourite source for stylish apartment furniture?

My absolute favourite source for small space furniture is ResourceFurniture in New York. They have an amazing collection of pieces that 'transform' from one functional concept to another. They have a wall unit/sofa combination piece that collapses to become a queen-sized bed – perfect for any apartment dweller. Here's their link – check them out! www.resourcefurniture.com

What are the most important furniture pieces to keep when downsizing?

I think the answer here is only the truly utilitarian pieces – sofas with only enough room for the number of people living in the space, one super-comfortable chair, and a bed ... just the things you NEED!

I've advised friends to look around their homes and assess if they've used something in the last ten days, and if not, they don't need it.

What is your number one tip for de-cluttering?

That's an easy one! I study Tibetan Buddhism, and reading about not having attachments to our belongings is key. Here's a great book, available through Amazon, if you'd like to learn more: *Parting from the Four Attachments* by His Holiness Sakya Trizin.

How do you optimise storage in a small space?

I think I learned most of what I know about optimising storage from my time working with Martha Stewart. She helped me to understand that carefully dividing storage space into areas/ compartments that suit the items being stored were key – there's not an inch of my Manhattan closets that isn't utilised!

What is your number one tip to make a small space look larger?

Reflective finishes always help, and natural light. If at all possible avoid window treatments – let the sun in and allow the outdoors to be visually accessible from your home. We perceive the outdoors as expansive, even in a big city.

How do you quickly spruce up a room?

When I was a little boy my grandmother always rearranged the furniture twice a year. She also had what she called 'winter colours' and 'summer colours' for the accessories, which she switched out from the attic. I also change the bath towels, pillows, and even the air freshener scent.

Where do you go for bargains and fabulous finds?

I'm lucky living in New York; there are many wonderful flea markets to shop! But I also love eBay, Etsy, and One Kings Lane.

What is the best decorating advice you've ever heard and who gave it to you?

When Marian McEvoy was the editor at *House Beautiful* she told me to trust my instincts. I try to always remember that.

What are your three sources of inspiration you can't live without?

So hard to choose! First I'd have to say the Metropolitan Museum of Art in NYC – endless colour schemes in works of art! Second, I'd say Style.com, because I think fashion and interior design are inextricably related, and third my imagination. The smallest detail, the colour of light coming through a window – my mind remembers these things and I interpret them into my work.

What is your favourite website for interior design and decorating tips?

Another very difficult choice, but I'd have to say Remodelista (www.remodelista.com), there's always something amazing!

James Treble is a qualified colour consultant with over 20-years experience in varied roles within the building and design industry. He combines his experience and expertise with his love of housing. This culminated in the creation of Treble Studios, which he has owned and operated since 2005. His experience within the real estate industry, new home building and renovating, as well as in the kitchen and bathroom design fields, enables him to offer educated yet holistic solutions. James is also the Chairman of Colour Society of Australia, NSW Division, and regularly features on Channel 10's exciting lifestyle show *The Living Room* as the expert interior designer.

What is your favourite source for stylish apartment furniture?

I usually work closely with my clients, and as every job is different in its style, so too is its suppliers. I basically work around Alexandria and Surry Hills for key pieces but also go wider for interesting art or unique furniture pieces.

These days I also use the web a lot and love Temple&Webster (www.templeandwebster.com.au) as well as Zanui (www.zanui.com.au) for their great range of interesting, well priced, quality furniture and accessories.

What are the most important furniture pieces to keep when downsizing?

To keep a sense of your own history it is always important to keep a couple of key pieces that have been with you over the years! It's always dependent upon the size of your new space. However, that comfy armchair, or small set of drawers, which can be reused as a bedside table or storage in a small hallway, are important to keep a sense of 'you' and help you feel familiar in your new abode.

What is your number one tip for de-cluttering?

For me, the fewer surfaces I have the better! I manage to fill every table top and bookshelf I have, mainly due to a busy work schedule and perhaps I am a little bit of a collector more than a hoarder! So I ensure I have pieces with great storage but less open space to fill up! Having said that, yesterday I was shopping for clients and managed to buy two cushions for myself. I didn't need them but they were so nice and a great price!

How do you optimise storage in a small space?

Go vertical! I have learnt over the years, and also from time living in a small flat in London, that floor space may be small but you can always use the vertical height in any space. Tall but narrow shelves, wall mounted storage, and built-in cabinets and kitchen wall units must go as high as is practical.

What is your number one tip to make a small space look larger?

Light ceilings! Colour is always the cheapest and easiest way to change any space. Although crisp white is a favourite, any shade of light colour will always assist in pushing ceilings up and making a space feel more open and therefore larger!

How do you quickly spruce up a room?

The simplest things to change are accessories and soft furnishings! Cushions, throws, bedspreads, towels, even a new lamp. Depending upon the room, changing colours and styles in these areas is always cost effective, has instant appeal and transforms the look and feel of a space.

Where do you go for bargains and fabulous finds?

That's a big question. It really depends upon the look I am going for and also on the budget of the client. But for me I love salvaging and finding new uses for furniture and objects that would otherwise be discarded. My lounge is a 70s long 4-seater with classic narrow arms! I used to sit on this as a kid at my best friend's house. He later inherited it when he got married but their cat damaged the fabric so they replaced the lounge. I gladly took the old one off their hands! The frame is solid hardwood with a sprung base. I re-upholstered it in charcoal fabric and replaced the base cushions. It is now a striking piece, which I love and everyone comments on. It would easily cost me about $4000 to replace, and it will probably go to my children!

What is the best decorating advice you've ever heard and who gave it to you?

Less is more! June Dally Watkins. I use it all the time and it relates to not only your interior but also as a guide to how much or how many pieces you need in a room. I like clean simple lines and strong statement pieces. I'd rather have one amazing chair or artwork, than lots of cheap looking bad quality pieces, which I will end up replacing anyway.

What are your three sources of inspiration you can't live without?

This is an interesting question, and I guess for me three sources would be:

Galleries – My partner is an artist and we regularly attend exhibitions and collect pieces whether in Sydney or overseas. This always gives me new ideas and inspiration.

Showrooms – Design and furniture showrooms change all the time and give great ideas for future projects.

Travel – I regularly travel for work and pleasure and, either in Australia or overseas, ideas in architecture or public spaces can sometimes be the catalyst for a great interior design idea!

What is your favourite website for interior design and decorating tips?

I follow a few sites for inspiration but I mainly love Houzz (www.houzz.com) and of course Pinterest (www.pinterest.com). Other times, for inspiration, I may randomly punch in keys words to find inspirational images depending upon the type of project I am working on.

Babette Hayes, interior designer and committee member of the Colour Society of Australia, completed her education in England specialising in interior and mural design. She started styling interiors for *Ideal Home, Good Housekeeping* and English *House & Garden* as well as writing cookery columns for *Queen* magazine and *The Telegraph* in London before coming to Australia in the mid 60s. Babette became Australia's first design stylist at a time when the magazine scene was changing. She soon became a household name as design stylist for *Australian Home Journal*, then design consultant for *Belle* and interior design editor for *Australian Women's Weekly*. She also ran a busy interior design studio and produced 14 books on design and interior decoration, as well as cooking, another passion.

Babette returned to London in the mid 80s where she lectured and ran courses and seminars in personal development and creative expression. In 1990 she came back to Sydney continuing with her private design work and styling. She writes freelance for *Vogue Living, Belle, House & Garden* and Domain Home in the *Sydney Morning Herald*, and keeps up her courses and lecturing in Australia and internationally.

What is your favourite source for stylish apartment furniture?

That's a hard one, I like several: Space, Koskela, Orson&Blake, Dedece, Ikea, and quality second-hand retro/Danish shops. I recommend poring over the top quality design magazines such as *Vogue Living, Belle, House & Garden*, and putting together a file or folder of your favourite pieces of furniture.

What are the most important furniture pieces to keep when downsizing?

Looking ahead to your change of lifestyle think smaller, keep one or two extra special quality items that you love, and carefully select your artworks to make sure they all hold meaning for you. Keep a good comfortable couch, it can be a 4-seater, a small dining table to seat 6-8, and chairs (they can be spread around), plus an ottoman or two.

What is your number one tip for de-cluttering?

De-clutter your drawers first (they are usually filled with junk). Then cupboards – keep going through them once a week to reduce by at least 60 percent: clothes, linen, bedding, china, bookshelves. Only keep what you love and absolutely need.

How do you optimise storage in a small space?

Built-in storage works best in small spaces but it needs to be well thought-through. A wall of shallow 300 mm deep floor-to-ceiling cupboards with full height doors takes an amazing amount of stuff, in a hallway or against a kitchen wall.

What is your number one tip to make a small space look larger?

Always keep it tidy. Looking at those glossy interiors you'll notice they have a sense of order and spaciousness, however small. Order and calm with everything in its place is a Zen approach that creates space.

How do you quickly spruce up a room?

Make sure everything is in its place, add a bunch of fresh leaves or flowers in a vase; make sure the room is well lit and feels welcoming.

Where do you go for bargains and fabulous finds?

Haunt the auction rooms, check out the sales, keep familiarising yourself with what is available on the web, check out stylists' haunts.

What is the best decorating advice you've ever heard and who gave it to you?

Keep it simple, be true to yourself and always love what you do – stop when you don't. Marion Hall Best

What are your three sources of inspiration you can't live without?

I enjoy the best of the design and architecture magazines, as they are full of inspirational articles, visual imagery and in-depth interviews. And I couldn't live without my collection of books on architecture and design going back over the past 120 years.

What is your favourite website for interior design and decorating tips?

I don't have a preference. I like to have a range of references from the latest offbeat to the elegantly modern to the funky and controversial.

Storage Solutions for Small Spaces

Scenario

Pam and Jack lived in a 4-bedroom house with a large garden in Brisbane until Jack got a job offer in Melbourne. Both in their fifties, they decided to downsize to an inner-city 3-bedroom apartment not far from Jack's office. Before moving, they passed on a lot of furniture and tools to their children. However, they have a large collection of books and beloved pieces they want to display in their new home. Functional storage space has a high priority for them.

No matter where you live and how large or small your home is, storage is a major topic for homeowners. To store and display books and cherished collections, there are a few options to consider.

In Pam and Jack's case I would recommend to work with the apartment floor plan and see if there is the possibility of building in a floor to ceiling shelf in the living area. This is a space where they will spend a lot of time and it is nice to surround yourself with the things you love.

A bookshelf can become a stylish focal point in your new apartment when effectively curated (see Step 5). Bookshelves can be integrated in any room where you would like your books to be.

Transform a long and narrow hallway into a library or build a shelf around your bed. Bookshelves also work well around doors to use the wall space above the door. Even a guest room can benefit from a shelf: offer your guests material to read, pile up nice storage boxes for keeping little things and use it to display decorative items. If your books do not all fit in one area, distribute them to different rooms of your apartment. Books have the most impact in interior styling and make your space personal.

Storage solutions for small spaces is one of the hot topics for apartment downsizers. Even if you have optimised your de-cluttering project, there will always be the need for storage in your new home. The trick is not to start buying too much new stuff and start cluttering your new home. Always keep in mind that you are aiming to simplify your life to be able to free up time for travelling, entertaining and enjoying your new apartment lifestyle.

Generally speaking, storage can be found in the most unlikely of places. Think of built-ins under stairs, a floor to ceiling bookshelf along a narrow hallway, full-height storage cabinets in nooks, drawers or open shelves under your bed. In his *Manual of Dwelling*, Kevin McCloud even suggests to lower a bathroom ceiling to create extra overhead storage space.

When you start planning your rooms, incorporate adequate storage solutions in your room layout. Think about what you want to keep in a certain space and work out how you can store or display your belongings. Depending on this analysis start looking for appropriate storage units. Compare customised built-in solutions with standard options available in the mainstream retail outlets. Take the time to do your research, as storage doesn't have to be boring. Luckily, there are great solutions out there proving that function and style can go hand in hand.

'Plan your work for today and every day,

and then work to your plan.'

– Margaret Thatcher

Hall/Entrance

A chest of drawers or a hall table with drawers can do magic in hiding all the things you need on a daily basis: keys, glasses, phones, camera, notes, pens etc. Allocate a dedicated place for each item. Depending on the size of your drawers, buy drawer organisers to keep things sorted.

I use an antique wardrobe, which I inherited from my grandmother for all our jackets, coats, bags and hats. This keeps the entrance clutter free and at the same time works as a focal point in this space. If you can't fit in a wardrobe use a stylish hallstand or wall hooks to hang your jackets and bags.

Under stair storage is a great solution for dual-level apartments. Consider a custom-made built-in solution. We had this done in our house and the amount of stuff we can store under the stairs is amazing! We keep all our shoes here instead of using up space in the bedrooms.

Dining Area

Apart from the kitchen cupboards and drawers, consider a sideboard with closed and open storage options in your dining area for keeping additional china and crockery and to display interesting objects. Keep your treasured collections or antique books behind glass doors in a gorgeous display cabinet. Share your collections with your friends and make your display a conversation starter while entertaining your guests.

Living Room

A multifunctional storage system can make a big difference in your living room. The trick here is to surround yourself with the things you love and hide all the stuff you don't want to see.

Wall-hung storage units are available in many different shapes, depths and lengths and can turn your organisation into a personal expression. With various types of finishes for doors and open-shelf modular designs, you can create your individual and distinctive wall piece. And remember, everything that is lifted from the floor will make your floor space look larger.

For your media equipment consider a closed solution to hide the TV and DVD player when not used. Cleverly designed coffee or side tables with storage underneath the tabletops make it easy to hide the living room essentials.

Bedroom

To get a good night's sleep, keep your sanctuary free of clutter and mess. Stylish storage can start with your bed. There are designs with under bed drawers or open shelves to store your things or display your books. Again, a sideboard is an elegant storage option for a bedroom. Bedside tables or built-in shelves behind the bed will help you keep your bedroom organised.

If there is no space for a bedside table, substitute a recessed wall niche for bedside storage.

If you don't have a built-in or walk-in wardrobe go for a highly modular wardrobe system to find a home for all your clothes, shoes and accessories.

Study/Guest Bedroom

Use a versatile sleek console table with drawers to transform your desk into a dressing table for your guests.

A chest of drawers will keep your study essentials but keep the first two drawers free for you guests' belongings.

Use an open shelf for books, magazines and folders. Put all the little things in decorative storage boxes placed on the shelf. A tidy shelf radiates a sense of style and order in your space.

'Simplicity of life, even the barest, is not a misery, but the very foundation of refinement; a sanded floor and whitewashed walls and the green trees, and flowery meads, and living waters outside.'

– William Morris

Bathroom

Your bathroom is most probably the smallest room in your new apartment. How can you optimise the storage of all the stuff and little things you usually keep in your bathroom?

Use the space in your under-sink vanity for hiding stuff you don't want to see: toilet paper, cleaning products or your hairdryer.

Tackle your drawer dilemmas with drawer organisers to keep all your little things and cosmetics sorted and easy to find. Use small and medium-sized storage baskets or stacks of little drawers for creating order inside your cabinet – label all the baskets and drawers so you can easily find everything. Tiny items can be stored inside cabinet doors by fixing small plastic containers on the door panel.

Freestanding storage units like a drawer cabinet trolley or a storage ladder for your towels can be a useful addition to your bathroom storage. You can change the position of these units, as you like. Make them blend in with your bathroom colour scheme or use an accent colour to create a bathroom feature.

Use free wall space for narrow shelving to keep small towels, soap or other bathroom accessories. Use different compartments and small baskets to keep various items in an organised manner. A collection of coloured glass jars is not only decorative but can also hold little things, like cotton swabs, make up brushes, lipstick and other small items you use on a daily basis.

Create the ultimate relaxation zone with an open-shelf solution where you can display your towels, store your cosmetics in gorgeous storage baskets and display all the beautiful things you use every day. Add a small vase with a single stem flower to make you feel happy in the morning!

A Look Behind the Scenes

Anders Nørgaard is one of the few contemporary Danish designers who have received international awards and recognition. He has a unique talent for designing modular sofa concepts that look great no matter how you put them together, and he is behind some of the most popular and flexible sofas. 'I love sofas. They form the ideal gathering point in most homes and they are the heroes of the living room', says Anders.

What are the most important steps in your design process?

The creative phase, the idea phase and the phase of sketching. But while function and craftsmanship may be the starting point in my designs, it's the small bursts of details that make the difference. They refine the look and give it a distinctive personality.

What sources of inspiration do you use to design a new product?

I'm inspired by everyday life, first of all. Furthermore, I find inspiration within my surroundings, people, travelling and different cultures – well, actually, by living.

What is the story behind your products?

Function follows design. What makes design work for me is when function, expression and price are in complete balance. When there is absolutely nothing needless.

Which is your favourite piece for storage optimisation in an urban apartment?

Sofa sleepers – for example, the Stockholm sofa sleeper I recently designed for BoConcept – and bookcases, without any doubt! Sofa sleepers are ideal for small living, and the opportunity to customise it with a resting unit with storage, completes its job in a small home. Bookcases, because they can hold everything from books to gadgets, papers, pencils, chargers, accessories etc. They help to create order, which is essential in every modern home.

Which is your favourite website for interior design?

The architecture and design site Dezeen (www.dezeen.com).

How and Where to Display Books

For booklovers and collectors I absolutely recommend a floor to ceiling shelf to create an inspiring and decorative living room display. To make it even more interesting, choose one with different sized compartments. Alternatively, build a bookshelf along the walls and around a door and use the wall space above the door to keep your books.

Another method is creating a library in a hallway and lining the walls with books to optimise this space. When using thin shelves within a frame, you can arrange your books on their sides to create an effect of unsupported stacks.

Think about a bookshelf in your dining room to curate your books and beautiful things you want to surround yourself with. Use your display as a conversation starter for your guests.

I love the innovative solution from a London-based architect who created a staircase for books to solve a big book storage problem in a small space. The staircase did not actually lead to a level above, it only made the access to the massive book collection easier.

If you have a corner between two windows, build in a corner shelf to ceiling height.

Use the wall space under a window for a narrow shelf.

Use a spinning rack like you find in libraries to fill a corner with books.

Buy a freestanding vertical bookshelf for any room you would like to have your books in.

There are some clever lounges with built-around shelving. This makes an interesting freestanding furniture piece to store books and display your favourite objects on the top shelf around the lounge. Additionally, the side panels function as a table.

If you have a reading nook, build a customised bookshelf around it.

Think of connecting beams along the ceiling with a timber panel, which serves as a shelf.

Read more about how to curate your bookshelf in Step 5. Check out my Pinterest board *Book Storage for Apartment Downsizers* for inspiration galore.

Toolbox

☐   Elements & Principles of Design Chart

☐   Tips & Tricks – Colour in Interiors

☐   Colour Wheel

☐   Colour Manipulation Chart

☐   Tips & Tricks – Tonal Manipulation

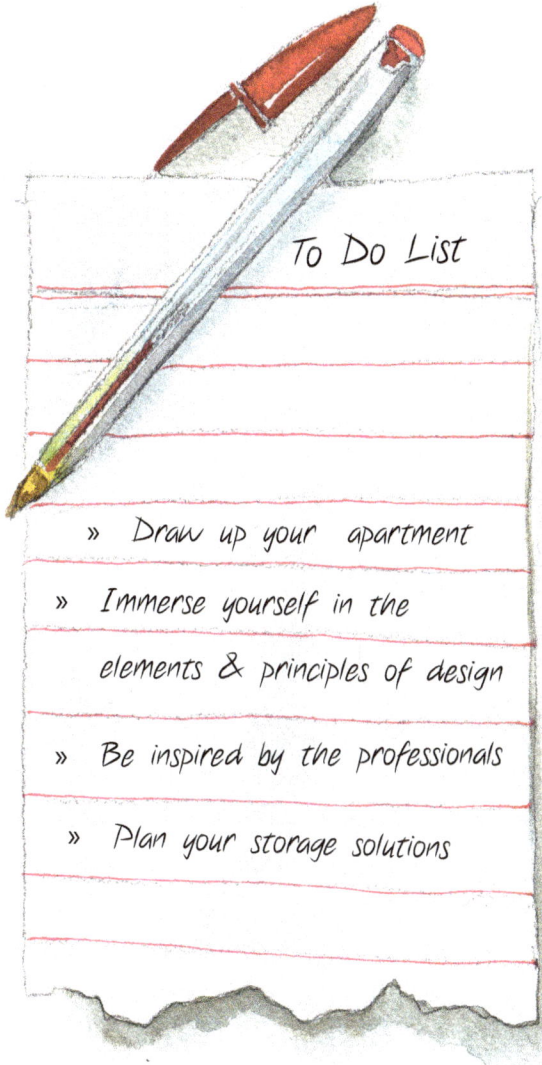

To Do List

» Draw up your apartment

» Immerse yourself in the elements & principles of design

» Be inspired by the professionals

» Plan your storage solutions

Step 5: Start Decorating

Mix & Match

Scenario

Lesley and Peter have lived in Europe for five years and are now moving back to Australia. Before they left they sold their house on Sydney's Northern Beaches and the majority of their furniture as they decided to downsize to an apartment after their return. A few favourite pieces went into storage. During their time in Europe they bought a few antiques and gathered quite a few travel souvenirs. Back in Australia they move into a 3-bedroom apartment in the area where they lived previously as they enjoy the lifestyle and proximity to the ocean. They would like to use their stored furniture together with their new pieces in their new apartment. They are not sure if this is going to work thinking it might 'look all over the place'.

I think this is a very exciting situation as mixing and matching different furniture pieces, styles, shapes, textures and price points can create a super personal home with lots of character and atmosphere: a home with heart and personality as I like to call it.

Before starting to decorate it is important to measure and layout the space to be able to work out what fits where. Based on your measurements you can easily decide on which pieces to go in which area or room. Once you have placed all your furniture in one space, start looking for a common thing: is there a colour that repeats in different pieces? For example, use an accent colour from a piece of art, cushions or a feature chair to link your space. If you have a lot of colour and pattern going on in your furniture and cushions, use a neutral textured rug to define this area. In the case where your furniture is very neutral, play with colour and pattern in a statement rug. Choose your focal point (rug, feature chair, art, fireplace) and work around it.

Once you have put all your larger pieces into your different rooms, decide what you need to add to complement the interior. Think of small versatile pieces that can be used for different purposes. Side tables with storage option, ottomans with trays to convert them into coffee tables, room dividers on castors – there is plenty of stylish and practical furniture around. Take the time to research and find it. You don't have to finish your whole home in one week.

In regard to travel souvenirs, cluster and display them in one cabinet or shelf to achieve maximum impact. Alternatively, spread them in different rooms and decorate by colour, for example. Create a wall display with different objects in one colour scheme.

You will find that the things you like the most probably have similar colours or textures. This makes it easy to add, as new

things will automatically work in your interior. As long as they have a reason to be there, they will work. And the most important reason can simply be that you bought them because they speak to you in some way and you love them.

One day a friend of mine asked me how I would define my decorating style at home. I really had to think about this for a moment. I am a mixer and matcher and have gathered lots of pieces from all over the world over the years. I just follow the rule that if I really like something I will find a way to integrate it into my home. I recently fell in love with a small Art Deco side table and could not help but buying it. I had no idea where to put it – we don't have any other Art Deco furniture, but I just love this decorating style. When I got my table delivered it was standing in the hall for a few days until I found a place for it in our living room. I needed to move a bookshelf (which of course involved taking all the books out), but after cleaning, repositioning and redecorating the bookshelf, I found I had a nice corner for my new table.

If you would like to inject your personality into your new apartment, mixing and matching is a good way to go: mix old and new, very expensive and very cheap, colours and neutrals. Be courageous and mix styles, price points, textures and pieces from different origins and eras to create your unique interior. An eclectic style is far more interesting and personal than living in a house that looks like a display home.

With your style board, and knowing what you love, things will come to you automatically. I have gathered lots of different objects and pieces from flea markets and antique centres, and when I see something I know that this piece is going to fit into a certain room. And as I have mentioned earlier, you will find a pattern and realise that all your pieces and objects will work together.

Mix squares with circles to break the monotony of the square shape throughout our homes. Usually we find a lot of squares or rectangles in our homes: square or rectangle floor plans, square lounges, tables and rugs. Break this pattern by introducing a round rug, a curved lounge, an oval coffee table or organic-shaped pendants.

Just follow the rule that everything you buy has to mean something to you and your interior will work. It is a simple as that.

Define Your Living Areas with Rugs

In a big open space use rugs to define your different living areas. Standard sizes are 160 x 230cm or 200 x 300cm. There are many rug companies who offer customised designer rugs with lots of choices for sizes, colours, patterns and textures.

A smaller rug confines a small space to read or work. For example, place a small round rug under a reading chair in a corner or define your workspace with a smaller rug under your desk. A large rug can be positioned under the lounge and the coffee table or underneath your bed.

Consider a large round or rectangular rug to define your living area. Play with different geometrical shapes to soften the look of your space. Place a round rug under a rectangular lounge and chairs and pick up round or oval shapes with side tables and poufs.

Layer Colour and Pattern

Have you ever heard of Kit Kemp? She is the queen of layering colour and pattern and her signature style can be seen and experienced in her boutique hotels (seven in London, one in New York City). Google her name and you will find several sources for inspiration.

Patterns are a powerful decorating tool and, like colour, can make a space come alive. If you like patterns and don't know how to incorporate them in your interior, start compiling a mood board. Collect pictures from magazines and take photos of patterns that speak to you while out and about. Additionally, think about patterns you liked in your childhood. Then, look at all your pictures and work out what the recurring theme is. Are you drawn to organic shapes, geometrical clean lines or intricate floral patterns? Find your style first and then start thinking about how you can incorporate the patterns in your apartment. A lot of patterns are linked to a specific period: think of the retro patterns from the 70s or the geometrical shapes from the Art Deco period. If you love geometrical and chevron patterns, use the Art Deco style as inspiration for your apartment.

'The person who doesn't make mistakes is unlikely to make anything.'

– Paul Arden

As a rule of thumb, keep your large furniture pieces in a neutral colour and add pattern through cushions, throws, lampshades, curtains or art. A patterned rug or a feature chair upholstered in a patterned fabric can make a huge statement in a space and may be a good start if you are not brave enough to cover an entire lounge in stripes or floral. Another important element is texture. Try and balance different textures: timber, glass, stone, velvet, wool, satin or linen. This will add energy and interest in your space.

Before you overdo it, start small and play around with different patterns in your guest bedroom, for example. Add a couple of patterned items, like a cushion, a lampshade or an artwork to your room. Mix and match different patterns and see how it feels. As long as you keep the colour scheme the same, you can mix stripes with floral, dots and geometrical shapes. If you don't like it or you feel something is not working, take away one piece and look at the arrangement again.

How do you know what to put next? Well, as most designers would say, if you only add a pattern that speaks to you in some way, it will have the right to be in the mix, and your interior will work. Go for what you love and make your space a home with heart and personality!

Don't go and buy everything in one go. If you love a particular pattern add it to your space and see how it works. Keep adding other patterned items step by step and build up your room. If you love a certain fabric think of having curtains made and a couple of cushions to link the space. Once this is in place, decide if you want to add another pattern – in the same colour scheme – to express your personal style even more.

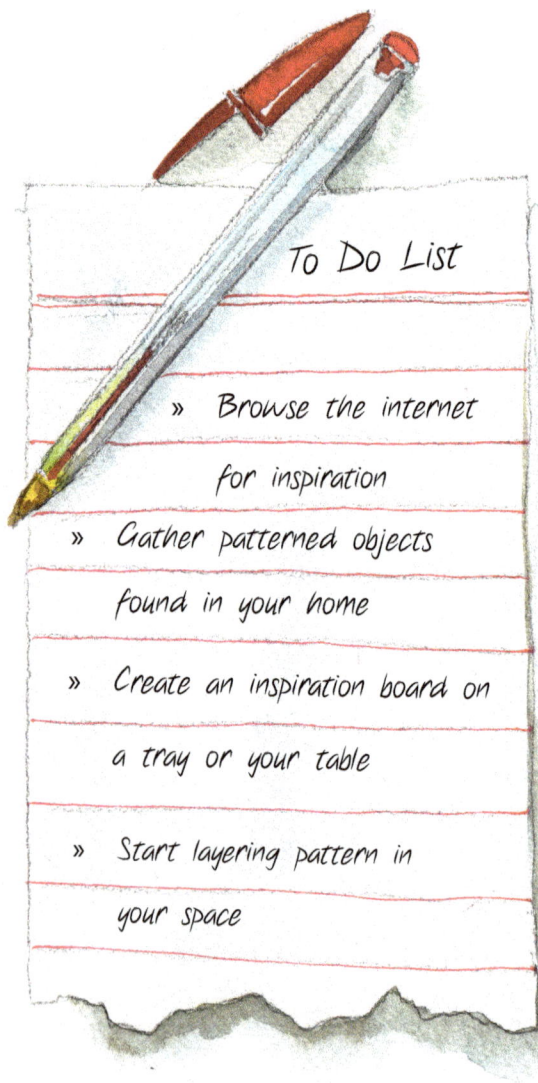

To Do List

» Browse the internet for inspiration

» Gather patterned objects found in your home

» Create an inspiration board on a tray or your table

» Start layering pattern in your space

Light Up Your Space

Lighting shapes the interior and can make a huge difference in a space.

Use lighting

* To define an area
* To warm up a space
* To create mood and atmosphere
* To add drama and interest
* To improve a working space
* To add colour and texture to your interior
* To illuminate your outdoor entertaining area
* To enhance the display of your art or collections.

Lighting design has to follow your needs. A 20-year old person needs less light to complete a task than a 60-year old person. The older we get, the more light we need to do certain tasks.

Always maximise the daylight in your home. When assessing your room, think about where you want to have the light distribution. Surfaces like walls, floors and ceilings reflect light. Think about the colour temperature of your light. There are fittings with warm and cool light available. However the more efficient LEDs are the cool lights, so try to find a balance between energy efficiency and the mood you would like to achieve. Research lights that use a changeable filter with which you can adjust the light temperature from warm white to neutral white. If you have the budget, invest in LEDs as they are more energy efficient and you don't have to change light bulbs. And they last between 15 to 25 years.

Consider an alternative to down lights. I have to admit I am not a big fan of down lights. This has firstly to do with the fact that I was raised in Germany where down lights are not as popular as they are in Australia. And secondly, I just don't see the need in having down lights spread all over the ceiling in every room. They are great in the kitchen or above working spaces where you need overhead lighting. However, to create a cosy atmosphere and an inviting space, a pendant paired with a couple of floor and table lamps will be much more effective than harsh overhead lighting with no focus. Sometimes, a cluster of candles can do the trick.

A chandelier over your dining table, for example, adds drama and defines this area and will create a focal point at the same time. With a dimmer to adjust the light you can't go wrong. I love the contrast of a stark white kitchen with a warm red splash back and three red pendants over the bench – stunning! Alternatively use fittings that throw light to the ceiling as well as to the kitchen bench.

If you want to set your display in scene, incorporate a table lamp or create a light source in front or in the back of your objects to add drama. Make table lamps a decorative feature on sideboards or consoles.

I am always amazed by the creativity of lighting designers. I found so many gorgeous lights that I started a Pinterest board about lighting design. There is a solution for every taste and budget. A stunning designer lamp is surely not an apartment essential, but it is a quality piece to save for and just nice-to-have, isn't it? And remember, quality design always adds value to your home.

Have Some Fireplace (Decorating) Fun

Do you sometimes admire the stylish mantel decorations in interior design magazines? Do you wonder where to get the decor and how to create something similar in your space – without spending weekend after weekend in shops trying to source the right items?

Relax and breathe deeply – it is not as hard as it looks like. Believe me. Decorating a mantel is actually a great pastime and a fun exercise. Use the things you already own and love and follow one of the two strategies below.

The first method of decorating your fireplace is to take the safe or more traditional way and go for one large eye-catching piece above the fireplace. This could be an artwork, a photograph or a mirror. This feature becomes automatically the focal point of your arrangement. If you have a mantel, decorate it with the same, or similar, items on either side to create a symmetrical look. Use, for example, small jars, vases or glass domes and finish your display with a couple of books at the end. Or place several objects next to each other in row centred underneath your focus piece. This symmetrical arrangement is easier to achieve and creates a more formal look and feel in your space.

If you want to try something different and unique in your home, I would like to encourage you to be courageous and have a play! Gather artworks and objects that mean something to you and start with one piece. Place it on the wall and keep working around it. If you don't want to fix it straight to the wall, lay it out on the floor and see if it works. Once you have found your starting piece, hang it on the wall and add other pieces step by step until you like your arrangement.

If you work with lots of smaller pieces on the mantel use one larger piece as a focal point to hold it all together. Think of different shapes, textures and colours when styling your mantel. Also consider the hierarchy of your objects. Do you want one piece to stand out and dominate? Or should they all have the same visual impact? And how do you want to align them? Step back and observe the overall look of your composition. And keep playing with it until you love it!

'A successful arrangement,

that is, an effective arrangement, is one

that powerfully engages your attention

and sustains your interest.'

– Leonard Koren

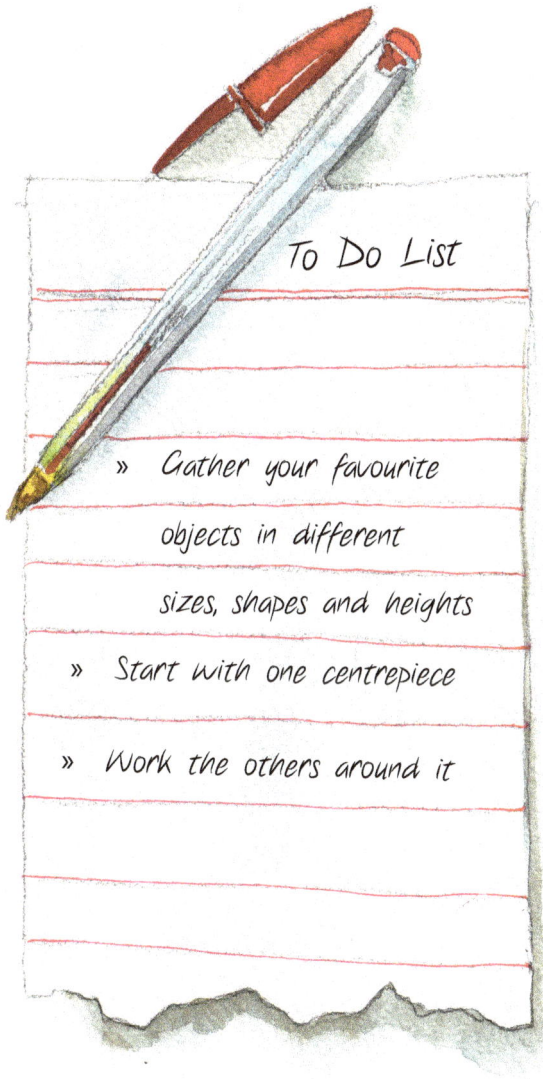

To Do List

» *Gather your favourite objects in different sizes, shapes and heights*

» *Start with one centrepiece*

» *Work the others around it*

The Art of Styling Vignettes

There are no rules when it comes to styling a vignette. A vignette is a placement of objects in a three-dimensional composition. It is a very personal thing and you can't go wrong if you follow some of the secrets of professional stylists. I have listed them below for you to get started and learn the art of arranging objects.

Tell a Story with the Things You Love

Use what you have and things you love to create an interesting vignette. If you stick to that rule, your vignette will work and draw interest from your visitors.

Play with Height and Depth

Build a composition that helps the viewer to follow your ideas and guides them along your arrangement. This is similar to the composition of a painting. Use objects of different height and size to make your display interesting. There is nothing more boring than a vignette where all objects are the same height!

Use Books and Flowers

Books and flowers have the most impact in styling. Build stacks of books and place an object on top of the books. Add fresh flowers, branches or a pot plant to create an organic look.

Integrate Art

Use a painting, photograph or a sculpture to make your display more interesting. Hide parts of your artwork behind other objects that sit in front. Use empty frames to showcase your favourite pieces. If you decorate a console or sideboard, lean larger works of art on the wall.

Work with Trays

You can't have enough trays in your household. They are truly versatile and can be used in any (and I mean any!) room of your apartment. Place different objects on a tray and they look instantly organised and sorted. Use this method in your bathroom, kitchen, living area or study.

Use the Power of Colour

Work with colour! Either keep your vignette fairly neutral, and add splashes of your interior's accent colour, or use one main colour throughout your entire display. This will link all your objects.

Trust Your Gut Feeling

And finally, trust your gut feeling! There are no wrong vignettes if you follow the tips above. A vignette is a very personal way of displaying your treasured objects and favourite things. Add and remove pieces and move your objects around until you are happy with your display. And a vignette is not a permanent thing, re-arrange and re-create as often as you wish. This is really fun, I promise!

How to Curate a Bookshelf

This is one of my favourite decorating projects: curate a bookshelf. A bookshelf doesn't have to be boring! The opposite is the case: a bookshelf can provide a room's biggest drama – especially when you use it to display treasures of all shapes and sizes, objects you love and art you can't live without.

If you have a large wall in your living area, consider having a floor to ceiling bookshelf with different size sections built in. Then treat each of the sections as a separate display. Place larger items on the bottom shelves and mix the smaller ones between your books on the top shelves.

Use some of the sections to only display books. Make your display more interesting by colour-coordinating one section and stacking some of the books vertically between others that stand horizontally. Add a little object in the same colour to finish off this section.

Place a small-framed picture or a sculpture next to a series of books in one section. Use another section to only display photographs. To keep small items, put them in gorgeous storage boxes and place the boxes on top of a book stack. Use a collection of vases in the same style or colour to decorate one of the sections.

If you have a lot of books, try and keep them in different places (see storage ideas for books on page 121 and create an interesting display in your main living area.

Creative Walls

Who says that you can only hang one artwork on a wall? Think of your wall as a blank canvas and find interesting ways to display your art or treasured objects. Especially in a smaller home, you won't have that many walls to display only one art work on! Group your art and find new ways to decorate your walls.

Have you ever heard of the French Hang? The term 'French Hang' refers back to the Belle Époque in Paris, when struggling artists used to pay for their coffee with a small sketch or painting that was hung on the café's walls.

The corresponding German term is 'Petersburger Haengung' or 'Salonhaengung'. The German words refer to the art gallery *Sankt Petersburger Eremitage* in Russia. All these terms describe the same decorating idea: a way of hanging artwork very close together – sometimes the frames are even touching each other. Clustered framing with almost no, or only a little, space in between was one of the trends spotted at the French interior design and home-fashion trade show Maison&Objet Fall 2013 in Paris.

The good thing about the French Hang is that it can combine different styles, colours and sizes. If you wish, you can choose a theme, a colour way, e.g. black and white, or group different works of art of the same size. Anything goes with this style of hanging art. And you can apply the same rule as before: if you like it, it will work.

Art is a very subjective matter and a lot of people seem unsure if an artwork will work in their home. When I worked in retail we had lots of customers looking for art for a certain space or wall in their home. And even if they had found a painting they absolutely

loved they were hesitant because they were not sure if it would work in their home. I always told them that if they really like it and it somehow speaks to them, it would work in their home. My advice is: trust your gut feeling.

Wallpaper is as popular as ever and the imagination knows no limits. You can even have your wallpaper printed to your colour specifications. If you plan to use wallpaper think about what furniture or accessories you want to use in your room. If you have coloured rugs and printed soft furnishings and lots of art and accessories, leave the walls plain otherwise there is too much going on in the room. However, if you love a minimalist interior, you could make the walls the focal point and decorate them with a gorgeous design.

For more inspiration, visit my Pinterest board *Creative Walls*.

Toolbox

☐ Tips & Tricks – Layer Colour and Pattern

☐ Tips & Tricks – Fireplace Decorating Fun

☐ Tips & Tricks – The Art of Styling a Vignette

☐ Tips & Tricks – Curate a Bookshelf

Notes

Tips & tricks

TO MAKE DOWNSIZING EASIER AND MORE FUN

How to Define Your Desired Lifestyle After Downsizing

Before you start looking for a new place to live, sit down and define how you, or you and your partner, imagine your retirement lifestyle. Think about what is important for you and what you want to keep doing after downsizing. This is an important step to avoid frustration after moving.

Take some time out, go to an inspirational place and answer or discuss the following questions:

* Do you want to stay in the same area?
* Would you prefer to move out of the city?
* What do you need to be able to continue with hobbies and interests?
* What is important to you in general?
* What would you love to do once downsized?
* What would be your dream retirement lifestyle?

How to Handle Emotions and Deal with Sentimental Items

Scenario

Jenny, 55, is living on her own in a small 2-bedroom house in Sydney's Western Suburbs. Her parents passed away a while ago and she has no siblings. Over the years she accumulated lots of stuff (she calls herself a hoarder) and paperwork. She still has folders with work from her time at university. She is now downsizing to a 75 sqm apartment in Perth, which involves an interstate move. She is overwhelmed by having to close different chapters of her life and say goodbye to lots of things, including furniture pieces she has inherited from her mother. She is emotionally very much attached to the few possessions her dad has left her. She does not know how to incorporate them in her tiny apartment and is very sad about having to leave them behind. As she has limited funds, storage at her new destination is not an option.

Handling emotions and dealing with sentimental items is one of the hardest things to deal with when downsizing. We project our memories in our belongings and feel we will lose those memories when we do not possess the belongings anymore. To overcome those feelings, the first step is to understand that our memories are NOT in our belongings, but our belongings trigger our memories. My mother died over ten years ago in Germany. I only have a few pieces from her that I physically brought to Australia. But all my positive memories are in my heart and therefore I will never forget her and the good times we had together.

Only keep things which you truly love and which trigger positive emotions. Choose one furniture piece, which you would like to take, brainstorm ideas (with the help of friends) and research design blogs online on how you could give this piece a new life in your new space. In the case of smaller items, incorporate them in an eye-catching display and give them a special place in your new home. Your parents would have loved to see this.

Learn to detach from everything else by seeing it as a chance to start a new chapter of your life. Pass on your beloved things to charities that truly appreciate them. I recommend relocation companies who have built longstanding relationships with organisations to pass on beloved pieces from downsizers.

'It is not how much we have,
but how much we enjoy, that makes happiness.'

– Charles H. Spurgeon

While de-cluttering keep the three questions in mind: What do I have? What do I need? What do I want? Prioritise and keep one thing of each of your parents, which is the most meaningful. Then think about functionality with regard to everything else.

To be able to make the right decisions, it is helpful to measure and layout your new space (see Step 4). Then you can work with a plan and see the proportions of your furniture in relation to your apartment. If it does not look right on the floor plan, it won't work in reality. This will save you time and money in the long run.

To deal with your mountain of paperwork, go through it and really ask yourself the question, do I still need this? If you have not touched it for the past 12 months, chances are you won't do anything with it now. Make a decision on the spot. This will free up your mind and let you concentrate on the future. Consider scanning the paperwork you have decided to keep.

11 Practical Tips to Deal with Sentimental Items:

1. Start as early as possible

Don't leave your de-cluttering process until the last minute before you move. It will be too overwhelming! Make a plan (follow the 3 steps to get anything done), show up and do it. Step by step, but consistently. If you can't do it on your own, seek help from the experts.

2. Scan/digitise papers and photos

Go through all your paperwork and pictures and decide which ones you would like to keep in digital form. If you don't want to outsource this job, there are free apps for the iPhone that turn your phone camera into a scanner, for example Genius Scan.

3. Pass on things you don't need any longer

Refer to Step 1 of *Downsize with Style* and your options for recycling and free cycling. Find someone who really enjoys and appreciates your piece. Put your unwanted things at the curbside to be discovered as someone else's treasure. Additionally ask friends and neighbours if they need your large household items. Schools and community centres may want some of your pieces as well.

Charities are always very grateful for functional household items and furniture. And they even pick the large items up. You only need to call them.

4. Take photos of sentimental items

If you have sentimental items you can't take with you to your new home because of the size, try and find a way to capture them: start a memory journal where you keep a picture and write a story about this special piece. This not only keeps your memories alive, you can share this journal with family and friends.

5. Prioritise the meaningful and functional

To help you sort out the most meaningful things, ask yourself the question: if I could only take one piece of furniture/book/clothing/china, what would it be? Try to choose one item from everyone who was important to you. Then look at all the other items in the light of their functionality in your new home.

6. Be creative

Think about how you could use a larger piece of furniture for a different purpose. An antique wardrobe could be used in your entrance hall for your jackets, bags and umbrellas. Convert an inherited chest of drawers into a storage unit for your study. Mix and match old chairs around your dining table for an eclectic look. If you have clothes you can't part with, use parts of them to make a quilt or wall decoration.

7. Chuck the rest

Pick the few things that really matter and let the rest go. Learn to make quick decisions: do you really need the collection of holiday cards? What about old paperwork, high school folders, diaries, photos that aren't really special?

Letting go of things can free up your mind and make space for new and exciting experiences. Practise how to detach (a constant exercise in my yoga class!).

8. Measure and layout your new home

Refer to Step 4 of *Downsize with Style* and measure your new space. Draw up your rooms and furniture and you will know exactly what will fit and what will not. Start seeing your move to a smaller home as a chance to create something new. See your new apartment as a blank canvas and use your mood board to create a new space for your new lifestyle.

9. Embrace your space

Curate your items in interesting vignettes. Display your beloved treasures and hide all the other stuff in functional storage units.

10. Don't start cluttering again!

If you buy something new, choose something else to go.

11. Learn to say no

If you have de-cluttered and are happy with less, tell all your friends about it. Use gift lists for your friends, so that they know what you need and would like to have.

How to Solve The Garage Workshop Challenge

Have you used your double garage as a workshop (your husband's retreat) or art studio (your favourite pastime)? And now, you are wondering where to move this favourite space with all its items when downsizing to a smaller home with no garage, or an apartment with one allocated underground car space. Can you relate to this?

This is actually an important topic to discuss before downsizing. Your workshop or studio is a vital part of your current lifestyle and, if you intend to continue with your hobby, you need to plan and discuss how and where to accommodate the activities undertaken in this space.

But don't get frustrated because you think you will have to give up these activities. Focus on the opportunities your downsizing decision will bring. Consider renting an empty garage or a creative space in a large factory-style building. Ask friends, or find like-minded people via your local newspaper, and offer to share a space with them. You will kill two birds with one stone: cutting the cost of rent and finding new friends with the same hobby. Embrace the change!

How to Keep Track of Your Family History

If you have grandchildren, write down the story of your life. They will be very grateful for it some day. My mother-in-law has a very interesting life story to tell, but she does not want to commit it to paper as she thinks that no one would be interested in it. Every time she speaks about her life to other people, they encourage her by saying, 'You should write that down'. And I believe, she

should. Especially for her grandchildren – I am pretty sure our kids would love to read it one day. So, if you have the time and are willing to make the effort, go for it! And you never know, there could be a book on the horizon!

Questions to get started:

* How did your parents meet?
* Where did you grow up?
* What was an important event in your childhood?
* How did you and your husband meet?
* Where did you spend most of your life?
* What did you do as a profession?
* What is important to you in your life?

How to Downsize with Pets

Downsizing and moving can be stressful — not only for yourself, but also for your four legged family member. If you are planning to downsize with a cat or dog you may have some concerns about to how they will cope with the move. But, as with everything else, a plan will help you overcome these issues and help your pet to get used to their new environment.

Plan enough time for yourself and your pet to gradually increase the time your pet spends indoors. Consider leaving your pet at home when you leave the house. Work on reducing time your pet is spending unsupervised outdoors.

It is important to get your pet used to their new routines as early as possible. If you move from a freestanding house with a large garden to an apartment where your pet can't get outside that often, start restricting outdoor activities before the move. Devote

time every day to your dog. Walk your dog regularly and establish a routine for feeding times. If you can, drive your dog to your new home and make him familiar with the new area. A dog walker could be helpful if you can't do all the walking yourself.

Be aware of your new neighbours who might not be happy if your dog is constantly barking. Consult with your veterinarian regarding behavioural training if your dog is a barker.

Consider developing a pet support network and research online pet networks in your new area. You may find like-minded people who are in the same situation and happy to swap pet favours.

For cats it may mean teaching them to be kept entirely indoors. Most cats can readily adapt to living indoors.

For specialist help, contact your veterinarian or research online for downsizing with pets.

How to Find the Right Real Estate Agent

If you are looking for help to find the right home or apartment to start a new chapter of your life, look for real estate agents who specialise in downsizing and have a proven record of apartment sales. Your agent should research the local area and the type of housing option you are looking for. I believe the most important thing is that you connect with your agent in your initial meeting. If you don't trust him or her, look for someone else.

There are agents with a special focus on seniors, for example the Seniors Real Estate Specialist (SRES®). A SRES® is uniquely qualified to help seniors and their families with later-in-life real estate transactions. They also help with additional services when downsizing.

An Agent's Top 10 Tips When Planning Downsizing

I asked Linda Coskerie, SRES® and Principal of Property Focus in Sydney, to share ten tips for homeowners planning to downsize.

1. Make a Plan

Moving from your much-loved family home is arguably one of the most emotional and complex stages of life. In the lead up to this moment, it is important to map out a plan to suit your future lifestyle and needs. Take time to consider: your interests, financial situation, health, transport requirements, social interaction, preferred location and proximity to family and friends. Remember, everyone is different.

Alternatively, can you leave the move for a while? It may be possible to adapt your home to suit your retired lifestyle by simplifying access, safety and maintenance. In addition, there is a range of services that can give you the extra help you need around your home. These services include domestic assistance, personal care, meal services and nursing care.

2. Consider financial implications

An essential component to consider when downsizing are the financial implications of your decision. Chances are there is a good deal of money tied up in your property and being able to access that could affect the lifestyle of the whole family.

Firstly, can you afford to make the move? Can you afford not to? It is paramount to understand how selling could affect your equity in the property. Furthermore, how does it affect your pension, super and tax position? And, how does it affect your estate and your will?

3. Communicate with Family and Friends

When downsizing to senior living, you will need support at every step of the way. Communication with those closest to you will certainly ease the stress. Keeping family and friends in the loop might be enough – sharing your thoughts will relieve the burden of this momentous transition.

Not only does the downsizing process affect seniors as individuals, it can impact on the broader intergenerational landscape – a huge life change that involves the whole family, particularly adult children. By keeping the lines of communication open, you will be able to discuss any concerns with those who have your best interests at heart.

4. The Best Option for You

Depending on your unique situation, there is a downsizing solution to suit, and it is important to do your research. Roughly speaking, downsizers in Australia fall into one of three categories: Baby Boomers (born between 1946 and 1964), The Silent Generation (born between 1925 and 1945) and The Greatest Generation (born before 1925).

Similarly, there are respective housing options to explore from stay at home with in-home care services, to active independent living options, and low to high care aged-care facilities.

5. Choosing the Right Real Estate Agent

In order to achieve the best price for your home and make a smooth transition to senior living, you should surround yourself with highly qualified professionals.

First and foremost, an expert in seniors real estate is a must. One who can provide realistic valuations, deliver effective marketing, negotiate on your behalf and close the sale with an outstanding result. They must also be proficient in finalising legal and financial matters through contracts and settlement.

In addition, your agent must have an inherent compassion for their clients by employing empathy, discretion and trust. Follow your instincts – the strength of your rapport is everything.

6. Specialist Professional Services

To remove the stress from selling your home, your seniors real estate agent can utilise their associated network of non-mainstream professionals who can help along the way – many with specialist seniors experience. This can take the pressure off family members to assist or act as project managers.

These professionals include downsizing and moving experts, financial planners, elder law and retiree services, seniors buyers agents, aged-care placement consultants, and an assortment of other seniors-focussed services.

7. De-cluttering Your Home

For many downsizers, the most difficult part of the process is de-cluttering, that is, minimising your belongings. Not only can it be hard to part with treasured possessions, it can be harder to know where to start.

With trust and care, de-cluttering experts provide hands-on assistance in sorting through decades of memories and keepsakes to help you decide what you want to keep. As for the rest of your belongings, they can facilitate delivery of unwanted items to charity, auction, and other means of disposal.

8. Stay Social

When the downsizing process is complete and you are safely moved into your new surroundings, there are a few ways to ensure that the next phase of your life is a happy one. Being socially engaged is at the top of the list.

According to recent studies, those who stay socially and intellectually engaged live longer and healthier lives. The concept of retirement does not have to mean slowing down, quite the opposite. It can mean having a new lease on life – enjoying every day by staying active.

9. Stay Healthy

Being healthy also contributes profoundly to a longer and more satisfying life. Whether you like tennis, golf or cycling, being physically active can lead to an increase in energy. In combination with great nutrition, life as an active senior will mean a decreased risk of illness, and fewer visits to the doctor or hospital, allowing you to participate more fully in the community.

10. Stay Happy

Finally, take care of your psychological wellbeing. The emotional impact of downsizing can often be underestimated. Throughout the process, keep your feelings in check and talk about them if you need. Likewise, after the event, take stock of how you feel about your new home and lifestyle. If necessary, discuss it with your nearest and dearest. Although sometimes overwhelming, downsizing can be a positively life-changing experience.

How to Find Help with Moving

You are very excited about your new home and can't wait to get there! But before you can move in you need to move out of your current home. This can be quite overwhelming the closer the date of the big move gets.

You have gone through your de-cluttering process, you have decided to simplify your life and live with less (don't forget: less is more!) and you have done a great job in detaching from a lot of stuff to free up your mind. Now, there is only one more hurdle to overcome: the big move.

Look for relocation services providing practical support to people who want to downsize and move. There are also specialised relocation companies, who deal with downsizers on a regular basis and know about your special life situation. They provide checklists and useful tips what to think of when planning your move.

Checklist and Tips for Preparing Your Move

Use the following checklist with handy tips of pre-packing actions to prepare your move. Lorraine Cox from Downsizing with Ease has put them together to make your life easier.

Whitegoods and Appliances

* Food removed from fridge and freezer
* Appliances defrosted, interiors wiped dry and doors left ajar
* Fridge shelving, crispers and fridge magnets packed separately from body of fridge
* Microwave oven cleaned and wiped
* Oven and hot plates wiped over
* Toasters and grillers emptied and wiped over
* Filters removed from coffee makers
* Dishwasher emptied and dishes cleaned
* Washing machine and dryer checked for clothing and cleaned
* Steam iron emptied

* Batteries removed from cassettes, radios, clocks, toys etc.
* Items that belong to the house separated from those that are moving.

Your Pantry

* Perishables removed and food storage areas emptied
* All lids tightened – especially on liquids
* Items that are out of date discarded.

Those Little Things You Can't Do Without

* A special moving carton prepared for small and valuable items, such as TV and video remote controls, bed legs, shelf, supports, bolts, keys, special furniture brackets, manufacturers' instructions and so on.

Your Personal Possessions

* Sort and select your possessions for moving or storage, especially if you are moving overseas. What goes air cargo, what goes by ship?
* Don't forget to leave clothes out to wear for you and your family for the day of the move.
* Items you may need for your car when you're moving, especially if it's a long journey: pillows, blankets, food and drink, maps.

Things Not to Pack

* If you're moving interstate or overseas, remember to leave out for your hand luggage essentials such as your

plane tickets, passports, car and hotel confirmations, credit cards, cash, travellers' cheques and personal diaries.

* Property settlement papers, other important business or personal papers such as insurance documents, jewellery, mobile phones, laptop computers, and any power chargers you might need for your phone or laptop, should also be left out.

* Check for any dangerous or flammable goods in your house or shed.

* Drain fuels from the lawn mower and trimmer, heaters, lamps, primus stoves and BBQ gas bottles.

Your 'First Night' pack

Have a special box put aside for the things you might need for the first night in your new house, such as:

* Alarm clock, kettle, tea, coffee, sugar, mugs, spoons, basic cutlery, plates, can opener, large knife, scissors, rubbish bag.

* Bed linen

* Telephone and phone plugs

* Power extension leads and adapters

* Bathroom needs, medicines, prescriptions

* Your pets' needs such as leads, bowls, bed and food.

How to Set Up a Garden on a Balcony

I am not a big gardener I have to admit. But while researching for this book I found some great websites with a myriad of tips how to create a gorgeous garden on an apartment balcony. It can be as simple and as complicated as you like. It can be a very expensive exercise or you can do it for little money. Again, creativity is the key! Perhaps you can organise a plant sale from your old garden to finance some new pots and plants for your apartment terrace garden? Or, take some cuttings from your favourite plants and put them in your new garden, providing that the climate and aspect is right. If you research the web you will find great ideas for containers that can be turned into plant pots. You can find inexpensive solutions at flea markets, general clean-ups or second hand stores. As with your interior, use the power of colour with your flowers, pots and cushions to create an inviting outdoor area.

According to the experts there are a few things you should take into consideration before starting to shop and plant. Assess your outdoor space and write down answers to the following questions:

* How big is your outdoor area?
* How much sun (and consequently heat) does the space get?
* How cold does it get in winter?
* Is your terrace exposed to a lot of wind?
* How much care are you willing to give your garden?
* Is water easily accessible?
* What is your budget?

Ten Tips for a Beautiful Outdoor Area

I asked landscape designer Nadia Pomare from Stylish Gardens what to consider when setting up a balcony garden. Here are her ten tips to create a beautiful and inviting outdoor area. Her last tip is my favourite one too!

1. Water

Pots dry out very quickly, so make it easy on yourself by installing an irrigation system. This will drip water directly onto the root area of the plant when you turn the tap on. For a little extra you can attach an automatic timer so the pots are watered daily before you get out of bed.

2. Food

Your potted plants are totally dependent on you. So use a good slow release fertiliser, appropriate for the plant type. Choose one that lasts six months or more. Mark it on your calendar so you know when to feed again.

3. Planting Medium

Use the best quality potting mix you can afford. It needs to be substantial enough to hold moisture and nutrients for the roots as long as possible. In the ground the roots have a better chance and don't have the same space and nutrient restrictions as in pots — so give them what they need.

4. Pots and Troughs

Make a plan before you purchase your pots. Consider the width and height they need to be. Stand indoors and look out to find the best spot to place them. Lastly decide on the colour and texture of the pot. This depends on whether you want it to blend in with the surround or stand out as a feature.

5. Plant Choices

Not all plants are suitable for pots. Read the label. If combining several plants in the one pot choose plants with the same water, light and food requirements. Often plant growth is restricted in a pot so choose a slightly larger species than required. Work out how many hours of sun versus shade your balcony receives.

6. The Elements

Balconies can be quite exposed, particularly if they are up high. No matter how careful your plant selection is, the wind causes plant and root damage including stripping the foliage. Spray the leaves with an anti-stress product to help at certain times of the year. Choose pots that are not porous and colours that reflect heat if the sun is beating on them all day.

7. Microclimate

Aspect plays a major roll in plant selection, but each little area will have its own microclimate. Check for radiating heat from brick or metal walls, cool breezes from neighbouring plants, and damp or dry areas too. Or create a new microclimate by grouping some pots under a large fern.

8. Artwork and Accessories

Artwork is great for covering unsightly walls and creating interest. Be careful to choose wisely according to the style you want to achieve. Colourful pillows, throw rugs, candles, bowls and ornaments will add the finishing touches. Be subtle and remember that 'less is more'.

9. Furniture

Ask yourself what do you want to use this space for? If you are restricted with space, custom-built benches along a wall that tuck under the table can work well. Allow plenty of walking space around the furniture by choosing smaller items.

10. Secateurs and a Cup of Tea

My final tip is my favourite. Reward yourself each day by sitting with a cup of tea to admire your new balcony garden. Keep a pair of secateurs handy (mine sit behind a large pot) to snip anything that is spent or becoming leggy. You'll find that a couple of snips a day keep the plants compact and neat, and will keep you smiling and relaxed.

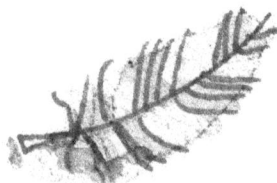

Follow Nadia's advice and you will be really organised and prepared when entering a nursery to start creating your new apartment garden. And visualise how much more time for fun stuff you will have when you don't have to mow the lawn anymore!

10 Reasons to Downsize Sooner Rather Than Later

Save Money

Save money by simply having less space to put furniture, TVs and electronic equipment, appliances or decorative items. Prioritise and only use what is necessary and functional in a smaller space.

Save Time

Save time by not having to do all the work in and around a large house. Start visualising what you can do with all your free time in the future.

Save Energy

Reduce your carbon footprint by using less energy for heating and cooling, and reducing your water usage in kitchen, bathrooms and for your garden. Contact your local energy provider to check out your savings.

Do More of the Fun Stuff

Free up your lifestyle and travel the world. Enjoy less preparation time when leaving your home.

Be Happier

Enjoy your new lifestyle with less chores around the house and more time for leisure, spending time with family and friends, and loving your home. Use a happiness journal to be happier every day.

Splurge on Feature Pieces

Get that one designer piece you always wanted and make it a feature in your apartment. Work out a clever room layout and make the most of space and proportion.

Become Organised

De-clutter, simplify, become organised and create an inspiring and productive space throughout your home. Creative organisation is the key to make the most out of your smaller space.

Be More Efficient

Enjoy being more efficient in everything you do. Make the most out of your new lifestyle through creativity and focussing on the essentials.

Simplify Your Life

De-clutter and simplify your life! Let go things from the past and make space for new and exciting experiences.

Start a New Chapter of Your Life

Be courageous and embrace the change! Make a decision and you will instantly feel better.

Toolbox

☐ Worksheet – Desired Lifestyle

☐ Worksheet – Family History

☐ Tips & Tricks – How to Deal with Sentimental Items

'A successful life is not a destination,
but rather a journey.'

– Chinese Proverb

'Twenty years from now

you will be more disappointed by the things

that you didn't do than by the ones you did do.

So throw off the bowlines.

Sail away from the safe harbour.

Catch the trade winds in your sails.

Explore. Dream. Discover.'

– Mark Twain

A final word:

BE TRUE TO YOUR DECORATING STYLE

As I shared with you earlier in this book, I love mixing and matching and have a very eclectic decorating style. I have always added pieces that somehow spoke to me, and never worked towards a certain decorating style. Our whole house is mixed and matched, accumulated pieces from my husband and myself when we moved together, antiques from my grandparents, contemporary storage pieces we added later, travel souvenirs, treasured collections of objects I find at markets, in charity shops and antique centres.

I guess, I am not promoting a certain style you should have in your home. I believe that everyone has a certain decorating style and my mission is to help you create a very personal, inspiring and happy home: a place, where you can truly relax and re-energise and eventually reinvigorate your new lifestyle.

The amount of information that is available to us every day through media channels and the internet doesn't make our lives easier. We are better informed than any generation before and we have to actively choose what we take on board for ourselves – every day. As you are about to start a new chapter of your life, have fun in choosing what makes you happy, and implement it in your interior. Be courageous and try new things. You never know what you will discover!

And, finally, enjoy the benefits of moving into a smaller home! Simplify your life with less stuff and therefore less stress. Splurge on some great feature pieces and work around them. Save energy! Stay organised with great storage solutions and enjoy your new lifestyle with more time for entertaining your friends in your stylish and inspiring apartment. View downsizing as a chance to create a happy home and boost your new lifestyle!

What Comes Next?

Now that you have read this book, I truly hope that you are inspired and enthusiastic to step out of your comfort zone and start a new chapter of your life.

Make a cup of tea, breathe deeply, and relax. Then, follow this easy-to-learn 3-step method: commit to it, schedule it and do it! Start de-cluttering using the strategy from Step 1 and you will instantly feel better. And even make money, if you are creative and clever! Keep working on your lists and head to www.downsizewithstyle.com to download your free worksheets, checklists and tips to manage your downsizing project.

Of course, if you feel you need some assistance for one of the steps, or the entire process please email me at Bettina@bdcolourdesign.net.au or check out my website www.bdcolourdesign.net.au to find out how my network of downsizing specialists, designers and I can assist you.

If you loved the tips and inspiration in this book, check out my HomeStyling101 e-course to learn about how to create a cosy and stylish home at your own pace. All you need to do is jump over to www.bdcolourdesign.net.au and register.

I also would love to hear from you, your downsizing challenges and how you tackled them! Email me about how you started a new chapter of your life and what worked for you. Like the Downsize with Style Facebook page and join my Facebook group Apartment Downsizers Sydney to connect and share with like-minded people. I can't wait to hear from you!

Bettina@ bdcolourdesign.net.au

Acknowledgements

A huge thank you to the interior designers and business experts for their contributions to *Downsize with Style*: Lorraine Cox (Downsizing with Ease), CJ Dellatore (cjdellatore), Babette Hayes (Babette Hayes Design), James Treble (Treble Studios), Anders Nørgaard (Furniture Designer), Linda Coskerie (Property Focus in Sydney) and Nadia Pomare (Stylish Gardens).

Thank you to Caroline Webber from Green Olive Press for coaching me along the writing process and to her editor for her valuable feedback on the manuscript.

A huge thank you to the super-talented illustrator Joaquín Gonzalez Dorao, who just blew my mind with his illustrations! He instantly understood what I wanted and translated it beautifully. Thank you, Joaquin, for translating my ideas into stunning visuals.

To Sanela Hromadzic, a very talented graphic designer from Sweden, for designing the book cover and page layout.

And finally, thank you to my husband, for supporting and encouraging me during the past months, and my gorgeous boys for their understanding that mum needed to work a lot to make this book a reality and could not spend as much time with them as they wished.

Do You Need Expert Help?

To find out more about the many ways Bettina and her team can help you create a happy home and refine your new lifestyle please visit her websites or contact her directly: bettina@bdcolourdesign. net.au.

Bettina Deda colour design

www.bdcolourdesign.net.au

Downsize with Style

www.downsizewithstyle.com

If you are after a passionate and creative interior stylist and designer with excellent project management skills, German efficiency, and going the extra mile to make her clients happy, then Bettina and her team of creative professionals and downsizing specialists may be exactly what you are looking for.

Bibliography:

Becker, Holly Decorate: Workshop. Aurum Press LLP, London, 2012.

Court, Sibella: Bowerbird. Creating Beautiful Interiors With The Things You Collect. HarperCollinsPublishers Australia Pty Ltd., Sydney, 2012.

Denning, Stephen: The Leader's Guide to Storytelling. Jossey-Bass, 2nd edition, 2011.

De Wolfe, Elsie: The House in Good Taste. The Century Company, New York, 1913.

Gore, Amanda: The Gospel of Joy. Head2Heart Pty Ltd., Chatswood, Australia, 2009.

Holloway, Mandy: Inspiring Courageous Leaders. The Messenger Group, Australia Square, 2011.

McCloud, Kevin: Principles of Home. HarperCollinsPublishers, London, 2010.

Morton, Megan: Home Love. 100 inspiring ideas for creating beautiful interiors. Penguin Group, Australia, 2010.

Salk, Susanna. Be Your Own Decorator. Rizzoli International Publications, New York, 2012.

Smith, Keri: How to be an Explorer of the World, Penguin Books, New York, 2008.

Urban Taskforce Australia: Urban Ideas Magazine, May 2013

Notes

Bettina Deda

About the author

Bettina is an interior stylist, designer, artist, colour lover and born organiser. She helps space-challenged apartment downsizers create a happy home and lifestyle through inspiring interiors. Downsizing is often associated with negative feelings and emotions. Through *Downsize with Style,* Bettina encourages empty nesters to embrace the change and be open to the opportunities that come with it.

She believes that only in a home that reflects your personal decorating style can you truly relax and re-energise. Therefore, it is her mission to help downsizers create homes with heart and personality.

Originally from Germany, Bettina moved to Australia in 2008 to start a new chapter of her life. Having worked in the corporate world for 16 years she downsized to start her own design business: **Bettina Deda colour design.**

In Australia, she enrolled in art classes at the National Art School and Julian Ashton Art School. She graduated from the International School of Colour and Design with a Certificate IV in Colour and Design (Award for Excellence) and a Colour Design Diploma (Highly Commended Award). She attended styling master classes with Megan Morton and Sibella Court, and a workshop on techniques for interior illustration at the Whitehouse Institute of Design.

In May 2013 Bettina launched her first fabric range for soft furnishings inspired by her hand-painted original artworks.

She has also released an ebook on how to successfully manage DIY home renovations, publishes a weekly blog, and writes freelance for design and lifestyle magazines.

A rare combination of German efficiency, excellent project management skills, and a passion for colour and interiors, forms the basis of her business and inspired her to produce *Downsize with Style.*

www.ingramcontent.com/pod-product-compliance
Lightning Source LLC
Chambersburg PA
CBHW051209090426
42740CB00021B/3426